The Human Rights Act 1998:
The Essentials

Callow Publishing

The Human Rights Act 1998: The Essentials

by Sam Makkan, Barrister-at-Law

London
Callow Publishing
2000

ISBN 1 898899 42 8

First published 2000

Published by Callow Publishing Limited,
4 Shillingford Street, London N1 2DP
Printed and bound in Great Britain by
MPG Books Ltd, Bodmin, Cornwall

Foreword

The Human Rights Act 1998 comes fully into force in October 2000, and its provisions will give effect to the European Convention on Human Rights. It is arguably one of the most important statutes ever passed by a Parliament of the United Kingdom. Our courts will be required not only to read legislation in such a way that the result upholds Convention rights, but also to take account of the case law of the Strasbourg Court; and it will be unlawful for a court of the United Kingdom to act in a way which is incompatible with the Convention rights.

So now we must read and learn the case law of Strasbourg, and we must apply the principles of the Strasbourg jurisprudence to the common law.

Indeed, we in the United Kingdom should be doing so willingly. For in 1950, when the Council of Europe adopted the Convention, the United Kingdom played a major part in the drafting of the Convention; the actual draftsman of it was Sir Oscar Dowson, a former senior legal adviser in the Home Office. And when the Convention was eventually signed by the Committee of Ministers of the Council of European 4 November 1950, the United Kingdom became the first state to ratify the Convention.

But there is a task ahead: in *R v DPP ex parte Kebilene* [1999] 3 WLR 972, Lord Hope of Craighead, at page 988E, said, "It is now plain that the incorporation of the European Convention of Human Rights into our domestic law will subject the entire legal system to a fundamental process of review and, where necessary, reform by the judiciary". Clearly, there is work to be done: one must get a good command of this law.

Some of the sections of the Act came into force before October 2000; and it is now a daily occurrence for the law reports to mention the Convention, on points ranging from over-reaching in trusts and disqualification of directors on the one hand, to covert surveillance and inferences from silence on the other.

For beginners and experienced practitioners alike, this book by Sam Makkan will lighten the load. He has the great advantage of having spent time at the Institute of Human Rights. So he brings clarity with his industry.

He covers the whole field: the Act itself, and the articles of the Convention, as well as the essential principles of the jurisprudence of the European Court of Human Rights. He includes a history of the Strasbourg institutions, illustrating with diagrams the present organisation. This is important for the understanding of the case reports of the Court and the Commission. There are references to the United Kingdom parliamentary debates, which will be useful for construing the Act, pursuant to the principle of *Pepper v Hart*. It is all clearly set out.

This is a first edition; it makes good reading, and it will repay close attention. I will take it to court with me.

J J Rowe, QC
Manchester
2000

Preface

The Human Rights Act 1998, fully in force from 2 October 2000, and the European Convention for the Protection of Human Rights and Fundamental Freedoms, are like no other legislation with which we are familiar. They transcend all areas of the law. Every aspect of our law is affected, from commerce to tax, to crime, to family, to civil liberties. Quite apart from the obvious historic, momentous and constitutional change, the Act and the Convention are likely to impact on all areas of law in a significant and substantial way. Our legal life is about to take a new turning. As Professor A T H Smith has observed:

"There can be little doubt that, through the enactment of the Human Rights Act 1998, the UK is on the verge of making major changes to its constitutional arrangements for the protection of rights, and commensurate with that, to the fabric of common law." (*The Human Rights Act* 1998 [1999] CLR 251)

Of course there has been constitutional legislation in the past, but the Human Rights Act 1998 is different. It is unique in its structure and in its approach to the Convention rights. Unique also in the sense that it simultaneously makes available the Convention rights in domestic courts yet seeks to preserve parliamentary legislative supremacy.

No lawyer, either in practice or in learning, can afford to ignore the Act and the Convention.

The traditional legal techniques with which common law lawyers are familiar will be seriously affected. We will all need to learn new ideas, concepts and principles, even before we begin to think of invoking a Convention right on behalf of a client. The jurisprudence and the methodology under the Convention and in the European Court of Human Rights at Strasbourg are wholly novel.

All lawyers will need to understand the structure of the Act and the Convention. We will need to become familiar with what rights have been accepted, and conversant with both the old and the new procedures of the European Court of Human Rights. Crucial to understanding the procedures are the admissibility criteria to be met before the European Court of Human Rights will even begin to consider a petition from a member state.

Even in the domestic courts, practitioners will need to be familiar with the structure of the Act and the Convention. In addition, if a lawyer is to argue a Convention issue, the lawyer will need to know the limitations on the Convention rights.

There is potential for the Convention rights to be violated by "public authorities". Lawyers will need to know what a public authority is, and what actions against them are possible for a breach, or a potential breach, of a Convention right.

One of the features of the Human Rights Act 1998 is that it is difficult to understand without a grasp of the basic theoretical and constitutional principles that underpin it. The book deals with the essential theory, to facilitate a greater understanding.

At the end of each chapter there is a checklist of the key points specific to that chapter. Readers can refer to the checklist either before or after reading the chapter, to identify those key points while reading, or to verify their understanding having read the chapter.

The new ideas, concepts and principles, together with the admissibility criteria and the structure of the Act and the Convention, are essential matters that this book deals with. It contains indispensable, basic knowledge which will be invaluable to all newcomers to the subject, whether in practice or in learning. It seeks to provide the basics, from which a deeper study of the subject can be undertaken.

Sam Makkan
Manchester
2000

Acknowledgements

First and foremost, my biggest thanks and gratitude go to my wife and children for their support and patience throughout this project. They have had to spend many hours, days and even weeks on their own whilst I remained glued to the PC or drove off to a library in search of material. I am eternally grateful to my wife for all her encouragement through the past months, and for the hours she spent in the early days typing the initial drafts, of which there were many.

The idea for this book was planted in my mind by my good friend and colleague Martin Fleming. I thank Tony Taylor for his encouragement and support. I am particularly grateful to Fiona Russell, at Policy Directorate, CPS HQ, for her in-depth comments, observations and suggestions on substantive matters at the draft and final stages of the book. My special thanks to JJ Rowe QC, not only for the Foreword, but for the very helpful suggestions on some aspects of the book. Last but not least, thanks are due to Philip Duffy at the library. He was always helpful in digging out cases and information when I needed them.

I was fortunate to have Pauline Callow (of the publishers) working on this book, giving it her undivided attention. I am grateful to her for her support and encouragement. I knew from the first time I met her that the book would come to fruition.

I dedicate this book to my family.

Contents

Table of Cases

Table of Legislation

Chapter 1

Introduction

Historical and Conceptual Background

Introduction

The origin and development of respect for human rights lie in the history of the interdependence of nations. Internationally recognised human rights would have little value if states could not enforce compliance. There is also the recognition that there are better chances of compliance if human rights are seen as the rules of belonging to a club of nations. Club rules stand a better chance of observance, compliance and enforcement.

Whilst human rights were developing in certain countries, the concept of national sovereignty prevented compliant countries from interfering in the internal affairs of other countries. Until the nineteenth century, the dominant view was that nations could deal with their citizens as they chose. But historical atrocities led to the acceptance of the view that a nation may be justified in interfering in the internal affairs of another nation. Thus there have developed minimum international standards of behaviour.

The European Convention for the Protection of Human Rights and Fundamental Freedoms ("the Convention") is seen as embodying those standards. The Convention, however, has its roots in another human rights document – the Universal Declaration of Human Rights (the "Declaration").

The Declaration was adopted in 1948, although it was only a declaratory document and was unenforceable. It lists a full range of rights, which fall into two broad categories: civil and political rights, and economic, social and cultural rights. Rights falling into the former category (freedom from torture, fair hearing etc.) are rights which states can confer upon their subjects and have power to protect.

The rights falling into the latter category (concerning housing, food/hunger, education and so on) are rights which to a large extent depend upon the wealth of nations. Because there was growing anxiety to establish rights which could be widely accepted and enforced, the rights were grouped into two covenants:

- the International Covenant on Civil and Political Rights ("ICPR"); and
- the International Covenant on Economic, Social and Cultural Rights ("ICES").

The United Nations adopted both covenants in 1966. The ICPR has been ratified by most members of the Council of Europe (see below). The covenant creates a Human Rights Committee which can require a member state to submit a report to it establishing what steps are being taken to implement the covenant. There is no individual right of complaint to the Human Rights Committee unless an optional Protocol has been signed by the member state in question. The UK has not accepted an individual right of petition to this Committee.

The human rights movement is not a European phenomenon but a global one. In Canada there has been in place for some time a system of enforcing the principles of human rights in domestic procedures. In New Zealand the Convention principles are available and enforceable in domestic courts. There are also the Inter-American Convention of Human Rights and the Inter-American Commission and Court of Human Rights. In Africa there exists the Banjul Charter, created in Banjul in West Africa. The Universal Islamic Declaration of Human Rights (1981) was proclaimed by the Islamic Council to mark the beginning of the fifteenth century of the Islamic era. Nor should it be forgotten that the European Convention has its roots in similar documents, proclamations and declarations prepared and adopted in haste in the aftermath of the atrocities in Europe during the Second World War.

The Council of Europe and the European Community
The Council of Europe, established in 1949 at the end of the Second World War, was part of the Allies' programme to ". . . construct durable civilisation on mainland Europe". Its purposes were to promote European unity, to observe human rights and to promote and facilitate economic and social progress. The Council of Europe is quite separate from the European Community. The Council was established on 5 May 1949 by the Statute of the Council of Europe. The European

Community has its roots in the European Coal and Steel Community, formed in 1951, the Atomic Energy Community and the European Economic Community, set up in 1957. They all merged in 1967. The aim of the Council was to promote European unity, while the aim of the Community was largely economic.

It is important to distinguish the various institutions and organisations. Thus, for example, the Court of Justice of the European Communities deals with issues and disputes arising out of European Community law, such as the Common Agricultural Policy and competition law. This court sits at Luxembourg. On the other hand, the European Court of Human Rights deals with issues arising from the Convention on Human Rights. This court sits in Strasbourg.

There are currently forty members of the Council of Europe, membership growing rapidly since the disintegration of the former USSR. The Council has its headquarters in Strasbourg. Its organs are the Committee of Ministers and the Parliamentary Assembly. It is largely perceived as having been relatively unsuccessful in promoting European political unity. Its most significant achievement undoubtedly has been the European Convention for the Protection of Human Rights and Fundamental Freedoms.

The European Convention on Human Rights
The European Convention for the Protection of Human Rights and Fundamental Freedoms was created by the Statute of the Council of Europe. The statute insists that each member accepts the principles of the rule of law and ensures that its subjects enjoy, within its jurisdiction, specified human rights and fundamental freedoms. Thus the protection of human rights is fundamental to the role of the Council of Europe.

The Council drafted the Convention based on those rights in the Universal Declaration of Human Rights which were thought capable of widespread acceptance and enforcement, that is, those included in the International Covenant on Civil and Political Rights (above). The Convention was drafted with speed and signed in Rome on 4 November 1950, initially by fifteen members of the Council. The United Kingdom ratified the Convention on 8 March 1951, being the first country to do so. The Convention came into force on 3 September 1953. The European Court of Human Rights was set up in 1959 in Strasbourg to deal with alleged violations of the Convention. In 1966 the UK accepted the right of individual petition. In November 1998 a full-time Court was established, replacing the original two-tier system of a part-time Commission and Court. The Convention now affects 800 million people in forty European states which have ratified it.

The Convention is an international treaty and is not directly effective within our domestic jurisdiction. Most European member states have incorporated the Convention into their domestic laws. In the UK the Human Rights Act 1998 makes available the Convention rights in domestic law.

The Convention is divided into three parts. Part 1 (Articles 1 to 18) lists the substantive rights protected by the Treaty, and Part 2 (Articles 19 to 51) deals with procedural matters such as the creation and composition of the court and the admissibility criteria. Part 3 deals with miscellaneous matters. The provisions of Part 2 of the Convention dealing with the judicial enforcement machinery were radically transformed by Protocol 11 to the Convention, which came into effect in November 1998. Protocol 11 has been adopted by all ratifying states. Prior to this date enforcement of Convention rights involved two organs: the Commission and the Court of Human Rights. Protocol 11 abolished the two stage enforcement organs and created a new court, although the Commission retained a transitional role until 31 October 1999. Article 19 creates a new and permanent Court of Human Rights. In addition, the Committee of Ministers has a supervisory and enforcement role. The Committee has many functions within the Council of Europe, most of which are unrelated to the Council's human rights role.

The most senior official of the Council of Europe is the Secretary-General, who is elected by the Parliamentary Assembly from a short list drawn up by the Committee of Ministers.

International Law and Municipal/Domestic Law

The position in domestic or municipal law is quite different from that in international or quasi-international law. In the UK, Her Majesty the Queen has what is known as the "treaty prerogative". In other words, the power to make or ratify a treaty belongs to the Queen, acting on advice from Her Ministers. Parliament plays no role in making or ratifying treaties. Consequently, a treaty does not, without more, become part of English law. Otherwise the Queen could alter or add to English domestic law without the consent of Parliament, which would be contrary to the fundamental principle of constitutional law that

Parliament at Westminster has sole monopoly of making or unmaking law – the principle of parliamentary legislative supremacy, or the sovereignty of Parliament.

The Monist and Dualist Approaches

A treaty is a creature of international law. There are two basic and distinct approaches to the way in which an international treaty is received into domestic law. These are the *monist* and the *dualist* theories of international law. The monist model is to approach both international law and domestic law as part of a single global system. Although they operate at different levels they are part of the same legal order. Under this model, it would not be offensive for a domestic court to apply treaty law in domestic proceedings where appropriate, assuming that domestic constitutional principles are not violated. An Act of Parliament ratifying a treaty would serve merely to make it applicable in the domestic courts. According to the monists, treaties are self-executing.

Under the dualist model, on the other hand, international law (treaties) and domestic law are two wholly different regimes. The concept of a single world or global system is rejected. Thus the existence of a treaty or its ratification in itself will not make it applicable in domestic law. If the monarch signs a treaty, the legislature will need to pass an Act of Parliament making the treaty part of domestic law. Such an Act of Parliament may transplant the whole of the treaty into the Act, or the Act may include a schedule which mirrors all or some of the treaty provisions. See, for example, Part I of Schedule 1 to the Human Rights Act 1998. Only upon the passing of such an Act do treaty provisions become part of domestic law. Treaties are not self-executing, a dualist would say.

Incorporation of International Law into Domestic Law

In countries such as the Netherlands the monist model prevails, but the UK adopts the dualist model. The most authoritative pronouncement of this principle – that treaties in international law cannot confer rights or impose duties in domestic law – is by Lord Atkin in *Attorney General for Canada v Attorney General for Ontario* [1937] AC 326:

"Within the British Empire there is a well established rule that the making of a treaty is an executive act, while the performance of its obligations, if they entail the alteration of the existing domestic law, requires legislative action. Unlike some other countries, the stipulations of a treaty duly ratified do not within the Empire, by virtue of the treaty alone, have the force of law. If . . . the government of the day, decide to incur the obligations of a treaty which involve the alteration of the law they have to run the risk of obtaining the assent of Parliament to the necessary statute or statutes . . ."

This principle was re-affirmed in *British Airways Board v Laker Airways Ltd* [1984] QB 142.

If a treaty requires changes to domestic UK law Parliament must pass a domestic Act of Parliament to give effect to that treaty requirement, for example, to bring domestic law into conformity, or to give effect to rights or obligations emanating from that treaty. A good example is the European Communities Act 1972, effecting UK entry into the European Economic Community (EEC) and making the Treaty of Rome part of domestic law by incorporating the treaty into UK domestic law. Another good example is, of course, the Human Rights Act 1998. If a domestic Act is not passed by Parliament, the treaty is still binding on the UK from an international law point of view, and the UK may be held to be in breach of its treaty obligation.

An Act of Parliament giving effect to a treaty in domestic law can be repealed by a subsequent Act of Parliament; in these circumstances there is a conflict between international law and domestic law to the extent that the former still regards the UK as bound by the treaty, but the latter does not.

In UK domestic jurisprudence there is, however, a presumption which usually allows the domestic courts to interpret domestic Acts of Parliament so that they do not conflict with treaty and international obligations. As an aid to statutory interpretation the courts have developed the presumption that Parliament does not legislate in a manner contrary to UK international obligations. See *Solomon v Commissioners for Customs and Excise* [1967] 2 QB 116; *R v Miah* [1974] 2 All ER 377; *Birdie v Secretary of State for Home Affairs* (1975) 119 SJ 322, *The Times*, 15 February 1975; *R v Secretary of State for Home Affairs ex p Bhajan Singh* [1976] QB 198.

So far as the UK is concerned there is clear difference between the effects of a treaty in international law and the effects of a treaty in domestic law. A treaty becomes effective in international law when it has been ratified, but it usually has no effect in municipal law until an Act of Parliament is passed to give effect to it, incorporating it into domestic law. The difference between ratification and incorporation, *inter alia*, is the key to understanding why it was necessary to pass the Human Rights Act 1998.

By way of contrast, the distinction tends to be blurred in some countries. In the vast majority of democratic countries outside the Commonwealth the legislature or a part thereof participates in the process of ratification so that ratification becomes a legislative act. This means that a treaty becomes effective in both international and municipal law simultaneously. In the United States of America, the Constitution provides that the President: " . . . shall have power, by and with the consent of the Senate, to make Treaties, provided two-thirds of the Senators present concur . . .". Treaties ratified in accordance with the American Constitution therefore automatically become part of the law of the US.

Although not hitherto incorporated into UK law, the Convention is not altogether alien. There is a wealth of case law already in existence where our courts have had to deal with Convention rights in interpreting domestic law. See *English Law and the European Convention on Human Rights* by Duffy, International and Comparative Law Quarterly, 1980 p. 585. There is also an argument that the Convention, or at least the rights that flow from it, are part of customary international law, which must, in turn, be observed in domestic law. In addition, it has been argued that the principles embodied in the Convention and the rights deriving from it are principles forming part of EC jurisprudence, and therefore have strong influence in domestic courts.

The European Community (EC)

A detailed analysis and consideration of the relationship between the EC and the Convention is outside the scope of this book. It is important, however, to grasp the status which the Convention and its principles have in the EC. There is a growing body of EC case law recognising that fundamental human rights are a general principle of Community law and culture. It is also now clear that the EEC regards itself as the guardian of respect for fundamental human rights. Much has been written on both these subjects.

In summary, therefore, the UK legal tradition regards international treaties such as the Convention as falling outside enforceable domestic law unless formally incorporated by an Act of Parliament. This has not, however, prevented the principles and concepts upon which the Convention is based from finding expression in domestic

UK law through the operation of European Community law, minimum international standards and the presumption that Parliament intends to honour international treaty obligations.

In *Nold v Commission*, Case 4/73 [1974] ECR 491, referring to earlier authorities, the Court of Justice of the European Communities (CJEC) said:

"As the Court has already stated, fundamental human rights form an integral part of the general principles of law, the observance of which it ensures.

In safeguarding these rights the court is bound to draw inspiration from constitutional traditions common to the member states, and it cannot therefore uphold measures which are incompatible with fundamental rights recognised and protected by the constitutions of those states.

Similarly, international Treaties for the protection of human rights on which member states have collaborated or of which they are signatories, can supply guidelines which should be followed within the framework of Community law."

For further enunciation of the above principles, see Case 11/70, *Internationale Handelsgesellschaft v Einfuhr- und Vorratsselle fur Getreide* [1970] ECR 1125; Case 29/69, *Stauder v City of Uim* [1969] ECR 419; Case 149/77, *Defrenne v Sabena* [1978] ECR 1365.

Lastly, in 1977, the European Parliament, the Council and the Commission adopted the following declaration:

"1. The European Parliament, the Council and Commission stress the prime importance they attach to the protection of fundamental rights, as derived in particular from the constitutions of the member states and the European Convention for the Protection of Human Rights and Fundamental Freedoms.

2. In the exercise of their powers and in pursuance of the aims of the European Communities they respect and will continue to respect these rights."

Indeed in the House of Lords, at the Report Stage of the Human Rights Bill (*Hansard*, HL, 29 January 1998, col 421). The Lord Chancellor (Lord Irvine of Lairg) said:

" . . . The word 'further' is included in the Long Title because, in our national arrangements, the Convention can, and is, already applied in a variety of different circumstances and is relied on in a range of ways by our own courts. . .".

Common Law and Civil Law Traditions

The Convention, its organs and the case law arising therefrom have their roots very much in the civil law tradition and jurisprudence. The common law tradition, by contrast, has been to adopt a strict approach, under which close definition of the scope and content of a statutory provision is sought. The Convention is quite unlike a UK statute. The Commission and the court at Strasbourg do not interpret Convention rights in the same way as English courts interpret and construe domestic statutes. We will have to become used to a different way of working. The Strasbourg court does not subject the Convention to a narrow, literal interpretation. It adopts a purposive approach, bearing in mind the policy behind the Convention. It adheres to policy and principles as opposed to literal interpretation and precedent.

Traditionally the UK domestic courts are prevented, by and large, from going behind an Act to ascertain the purpose of a particular piece of legislation. Those judges who have sought to depart from the tradition have been reprimanded in strong judicial language. One such judge was the late Lord Denning. His campaign over many years, whilst in judicial office, to depart from the traditional rules of statutory construction did not make him popular with his brethren in the House of Lords. Nevertheless, in certain circumstances, *Pepper v Hart* [1993] AC 593 alters the position to the extent that judges may make reference to *Hansard* in construing an Act of Parliament. Lord Denning's only regret would have been that *Pepper v Hart* did not come in his time on the bench.

The techniques, principles and approaches adopted in dealing with EC law are, it is submitted, the same, or very similar to, the approach adopted when dealing with the Convention rights.

Statutory Interpretation

This is illustrated in *Bulmer v Bollinger* [1974] Ch 401, at page 425, where Lord Denning described the differences between the English and the European approaches to statutory interpretation. The action concerned the use of the word "champagne" in the expressions "champagne cider" and "champagne perry". There was a request for the case to be transferred to the European Court for a ruling as to whether such use was an infringement of Community Regulations. The domestic court refused to make such a reference, and an appeal against that decision was brought. In the course of refusing the appeal, Lord Denning MR spoke of the nature of Community law and the principles of interpretation:

"It is apparent that in very many cases the English courts will interpret the Treaty themselves. They will not refer the question to the European Court at Luxembourg. What then are the principles of interpretation to be applied? Beyond doubt the English Court must follow the same principles as the European Court. Otherwise there would be a difference between the countries of the nine. That would never do. All the courts of all nine countries should interpret the Treaty in the same way. They should all apply the same principles . . .

What a task is thus set before us! The Treaty is quite unlike any of the enactments to which we have become accustomed. The draftsmen of our statutes have striven to express themselves with the utmost exactness. They have tried to foresee all possible circumstances that may arise and to provide for them. They have sacrificed style and simplicity. They have forgone brevity. They have become long and involved. In consequence, the judges have followed suit. They interpret a statute as applying only to circumstances covered by the very words. They give them a literal interpretation. If the statute does not cover a new situation – which was not foreseen – the judges hold that they have no power to fill the gap. To do so would be 'a naked usurpation of the legislative function': see *Magor and St Mellons Rural District Council v Newport Corporation* [1952] AC 189, 191. The gap must remain open until Parliament finds time to fill it.

How different is this Treaty! It lays down general principles. It expresses its aims and purposes. All in sentences of moderate length and commendable style. But it lacks precision. It uses words and phrases without defining what they mean. An English lawyer would look for an interpretation clause, but he would look in vain. There is none. All the way through the Treaty there are gaps and lacunae. These have to be filled in by the judges, or by Regulations or by directives. It is the European way. That appears from . . . the decision . . . *In re Tax on Imported Lemons* [1968] CMLR 1.

Likewise the Regulations and directives . . . They are quite unlike our statutory instruments. They have to give the reasons on which they are based: article 190. So they start off with pages of preambles, 'whereas' and 'whereas' and 'whereas'. These show the purpose and intent of the Regulations or directives . . . In case of difficulty recourse is had to the preambles. These are useful to show the purpose and intent behind it all. But much is left to the judges. The enactments give only an outline plan. The details are to be filled in by the judges.

Seeing these differences, what are the English courts to do when they are faced with a problem of interpretation? They must follow the European pattern. No longer must they examine the words in meticulous detail. No longer must they argue about the precise grammatical sense. They must look to purpose or intent. To quote the words of the European court in the *Da Costa* case [1963] CMLR 224, 237, they must deduce 'from the wording and the spirit of the Treaty and the meaning of the community rules.' . . . They must consider, if need be, all the authentic texts . . . They must divine the spirit of the Treaty and gain inspiration from it . . . They must do what the framers of the instrument would have done if they had thought about it. So we must do the same. Those are the principles, as I understand it, on which the European court acts."

Lord Denning returned to the theme in 1977. In *Buchanan v Babco* [1977] 2 WLR 107, a contract was subject to the terms and conditions of the Convention for the International Carriage of Goods by Road, set out in the Schedule to the Carriage of Goods by Road Act 1965. In the course of giving judgment for the plaintiff, attention was given to the Convention. Lord Denning said:

"This article 23 is an agreed clause in an international convention. As such it should be given the same interpretation in all the countries who were parties to the convention. It would be absurd that the courts of England should interpret it differently . . .

We must, therefore, put on one side our traditional rules of interpretation. We have for years tended to stick too closely to the letter – to the literal interpretation. We ought, in interpreting this convention, to adopt the European method . . . Some of us recently spent some time in Luxembourg discussing it with the members of the European Court, and our colleagues in the other countries of the nine . . .

They adopt a method which they call in English by strange words – at any rate they were strange to me – the 'schematic and teleological' method of interpretation. It is not so alarming as it sounds. All it means is that judges do not go by the literal meaning of the words or by the grammatical structure of the sentence. They go by the design or the purpose which lies behind it. When they come upon a situation which is to their minds within the spirit – but not the letter – of the legislation, they solve the problem by looking at the design and the purpose of the legislature – at the effect which it sought to achieve. They then interpret the legislation so as to produce the desired effect. This means that they fill the gaps, quite unashamedly, without hesitation. They ask simply: what is the sensible way of dealing with this situation so as to give effect to the presumed intention of the legislature? They lay down the law accordingly. If you study the decisions of the European Court, you will see that they do it every day. To our eyes – short sighted by tradition – it is legislation pure and simple. But to their eyes it is fulfilling the true role of the courts. They are giving effect to what the legislature intended, or may be presumed to have intended. I see nothing wrong in this. Quite the contrary. It is a method of interpretation which I advocated long ago in *Seaford Courts Estates v Asher* [1949] 2 KB. It did not gain acceptance at that time. It was condemned by Lord Simonds in the House of Lords in *Magor v Newport Corporation* [1952] AC 189, as 'a naked usurpation of the legislative power.' But the time has now come when we should think again. In interpreting the Treaty of Rome (which is part of our law) we must certainly adopt the new approach. Just as in Rome you should do as Rome does. So in the European Community, you should do as the European Court does."

Interpretation of the Convention

The word "binding" is the language of strict precedent on which a common law lawyer is brought up, but under the Convention and its jurisprudence there is no formal system of precedent. It is said that the Convention is a "living instrument". Social, economic, political, cultural, moral and other imperatives change over time, and interpreting the Convention is a dynamic process, taking into account such changes in circumstances. In *Tyrer v United Kingdom* [1978] 2 EHRR 1, the European Court of Human Rights (ECHR) said that the Convention must be interpreted in the light of present day conditions.

Although the ECHR is not bound by its own previous decisions it does not necessarily depart from them. There are instances where it would be appropriate to follow a previous decision. The point is that the ECHR is not *bound* by an earlier authority. Contrast the position with that of the Court of Appeal in the UK, which is bound by an earlier domestic authority even when it would wish to depart from it, unless it can be distinguished.

The Convention is intended to make available rights which are not theoretical and illusory, but rights and freedoms that are practical and effective: *Marckx v Belgium* [1979] 2 EHRR 330. In addition, the Convention is an international instrument to be interpreted in accordance with the principles of international law. Because it is an international treaty the Vienna Convention on the Law of Treaties 1969 governs its interpretation, providing that, in interpreting treaties, regard should be had to the central purposes of the treaty, and the purposive interpretation given to it. As we have seen above, the Convention has its roots in the civil law tradition. A glance at the wording of the Convention shows that it is drafted in the civil law tradition, establishing very broad principles, using loose and imprecise language. Any attempt to subject it to the literal interpretation would be inappropriate and would cause difficulty. It is submitted that the principles of interpretation that Lord Denning talked of in the two passages quoted above are the appropriate principles of interpretation applicable to the Convention.

The Interpretative Obligation

A key feature of the Human Rights Act 1998, dealt with here and, in more detail, elsewhere in this book, is what is known as the *interpretative obligation*. This obligation is found in the combined effects of ss 2, 3 and 6 of the Act. The most frequent recourse to the Act is likely to be for purposes of interpretation. The Act requires courts and public authorities to interpret both statutes and common law so as to be compatible with Convention rights wherever possible, notwithstanding (perhaps more literal) interpretations or precedents to the contrary.

Section 2 of the Human Rights Act 1998 obliges any court or tribunal to take into account the jurisprudence of the Strasbourg organs. (the Court, the Commission, and the Committee of Ministers) when looking into a question which has arisen under the Convention. Section 3 requires primary and subordinate legislation to be read and given effect to in a way which is compatible with the Convention rights, " . . . so far as it is possible to do so . . .". This requirement extends to legislation enacted both before and after the Human Rights

Act 1998.

Section 3 appears to be directed to anyone reading the Act and the legislation and not just the courts.

Section 6 makes it unlawful for any public authority to act in a way which is incompatible or inconsistent with a Convention right unless it is required to do so by primary legislation which cannot be read compatibly with the Convention. Section 3(2)(b) and (c) state that, where it is not possible to read domestic legislation consistently with the Convention, this does not affect the validity and continuing operation or enforcement of the particular piece of domestic legislation. Section 4 of the Act empowers the higher courts, in such circumstances, to make a "declaration of incompatibility".

Thus, the mechanism adopted by the Human Rights Act 1998, in the interplay of ss 2, 3 and 6, provides the key, it is submitted, to understanding the interpretative obligation. Whilst preserving the principle of parliamentary legislative supremacy, these three sections alter completely both the way in which the courts can scrutinise legislation, and the way in which judges are required to interpret common law. The Act is a subtle balance between preserving parliamentary legislative supremacy and providing a new approach to interpretation and legislative construction.

The doctrine of *margin of appreciation*, which is a principle of interpretation used by the ECHR, also comes into play; this is discussed at page 139.

As Lord Cooke of Thorndon said during the Parliamentary debates on the Bill: " . . . the common law approach to statutory interpretation will never be the same again . . .", and:

"section 3 will require a very different approach to interpretation from that to which English courts are accustomed. Traditionally, the search has been for the true meaning: now it will be for a possible meaning that would prevent the making of a declaration of incompatibility."

The White Paper of October 1997, *Rights Brought Home* (Cm 3782), which preceded the Bill, says "that the new rule of statutory interpretation will go far beyond the present rule. The judicial approach to interpreting common law will also change fundamentally."

Background to the Human Rights Act 1998

The traditional view was that the rights and freedoms embodied in the

Convention were and could be protected under the common law. In the last two to three decades there had developed an awareness and concern that the common law was not delivering this protection in the way hoped. In the Consultation Paper of December 1996, *Bringing Rights Home,* and in the White Paper, *Rights Brought Home* (above) it was argued that incorporation was necessary. Indeed in the 1970s and early 1980s a series of Hamlyn Lectures and certain publications argued for the need to formalise the rights and freedoms guaranteed in the Convention. In *English Law – The New Dimension,* Sir Leslie Scarman asked the rhetorical question, "has the common law come to an end".

There have been many attempts, in the past, to introduce a Bill of Rights. For one reason or another they have all failed, but the history of these attempts, and those who made them, is interesting.

Labour Party Consultation Paper (December 1996)
This document talked of "bringing rights home". It made the point that it was UK draftsmen who drew up the text of the Convention, yet it had never been incorporated into the UK law. This means that, except in limited circumstances, British people cannot invoke Convention rights before the British courts. This in turn means that:
- British judges are denied the opportunity of building up a body of case law on the Convention which is very much, and properly, based on British constitutional and legal traditions.
- The European Court of Human Rights has not benefited from the experience of the British courts or developed an awareness or appreciation of British legal principles and traditions. No practising British judge had been appointed to the Strasbourg court.
- Costs and delay: it takes, on average, six years from first complaint to the Commission to a judgment of the Court.

It was argued in the Consultation Paper that the most speedy remedy would be to pass legislation incorporating the Convention into domestic law. The Labour Party believed that this would enable the British people to enforce Convention rights in the UK courts and allow UK judges to apply the Convention principles in their courts.

In 1995 there was a 50 per cent increase in the number of cases brought under the Convention against the UK and held to be admissible. Overall there have been more than 300 admitted challenges to the UK's adherence to the Convention. The UK record is characterised by the serious nature of the cases brought, and the absence of speedy and effective domestic remedies. This record does little for the reputation of Parliament, government and courts. It affects the UK's international standing on human rights as well as disadvantaging individual citizens.

Apart from the above factors, there may also be a political desire to have a real and genuine influence in Europe. There can be no better way to seek to influence an institution than through its judicial and legal processes. It has been said that there has not been a better export from this country than the common law.

In the run-up to the 1997 general election, the Labour Party made a Manifesto commitment to introduce a Bill to incorporate The European Convention of Human Rights.

The White Paper (October 1997)

This document (Cm 3782) talked of "rights brought home" and introduced the idea of the Human Rights Bill. It went on to explain that the government saw the Bill and The Act as part of its "comprehensive programme of constitutional reform". The other elements of this programme are:
- the Scottish Parliament,
- the Welsh Assembly,
- a mayor of London,
- freedom of information, and
- reform of the House of Lords.

Thus, the Human Rights Act 1998 is seen as the delivery of a Manifesto promise, and a component of the government's drive to modernise British politics.

Checklist

Historical and Conceptual Background
- Second World War – European desire for peace and respect for human rights, although the idea has roots which go back to the Magna Carta.
- The Universal Declaration of Human Rights.
- The creation and adoption of the European Convention.
- The Council of Europe *cf* the EEC.
- Differences between the institutions and the need for clarity in distinguishing them.

International and Municipal/Domestic law
- Status of international and quasi-international instruments/treaties under the domestic constitution.
- Parliamentary legislative supremacy.
- Doctrine of treaty prerogative (ratification of treaty by the sovereign), hence the need for incorporation.
- Monist and dualist models of international law.
- Contrast position under, e.g., the American Constitution.
- Distinction between ratification and incorporation.
- Although not incorporated, the Convention is not altogether an alien or new concept; experience of customary international law and the EC.
- Presumption in law that the UK does not legislate in a manner contrary to its international obligations.
- Presumption allowing domestic courts to interpret domestic law so as not to conflict with UK treaty and international obligations.
- Case law to support the above.
- The Lord Chancellor's comment on the use of the word "further" in the long title.

Civil and Common Law Traditions: Interpretation
- The origins of, and case law arising from, the Convention have their roots in the civil law tradition and jurisprudence.
- Interpretation.
- Literal *cf* purposive interpretation (*Pepper v Hart*).
- Principles *cf* precedents.
- Schematic and teleological approach.
- Denning MR in *Bulmer v Bollinger*.
- Interpretation of Convention in accordance with its purposes.
- No formal system of precedent under the Convention.
- The Convention is a "living instrument".
- The Lord Chancellor's comment on the word "binding".
- Lord Cooke of Thorndon: "The common law approach to statutory interpretation will never be the same again".

Background to the Human Rights Act 1998
- Loss of traditional confidence in common law.
- Labour Party Manifesto promise.
- *Bringing Rights Home*, Labour Party Consultation Paper (December 1996).

- *Rights Brought Home*, The White Paper (October 1997).
- The government sees the Convention and its incorporation as part of its "comprehensive programme of constitutional reform" and modernising British politics.
- The Human Rights Act 1998 is seen as the delivery of an election promise.

Chapter 2

The Convention Institutions

The Old ECHR Structure

Changes to the structure of the institutions established by the Convention and based in Strasbourg came into effect in 1998 by virtue of Protocol 11 to the Convention. It is, however, necessary to look at the old structure in order to appreciate and understand its jurisprudence and case law which will continue to be relevant and which will be cited in UK courts. Section 2 of the Human Rights Act 1998 requires courts and tribunals to take into account the Strasbourg jurisprudence.

Two main bodies were responsible for construing and applying Convention principles: the European Commission of Human Rights and the European Court of Human Rights.

An initial complaint to the institutions at Strasbourg could not be made unless and until domestic remedies had been exhausted, and had then to be lodged with the Commission within six months of exhausting those remedies; and unless the petitioner was a "victim". The Commission ruled on the admissibility of the case, acting as a filter. About 90 per cent of petitions were ruled inadmissible. The exhaustion of domestic remedies was (and remains) an important rule. Once a petition was ruled admissible by the Commission, it went through a process aimed at finding a friendly settlement; this process is likely to continue under the new regime. UK lawyers must, therefore, be aware of the case law on admissibility and friendly settlements.

A friendly settlement would be sought once an application was ruled admissible. The process ran in tandem with the substantive proceedings. A friendly settlement is an agreement between the government in question and the petitioner. It may involve the payment of damages and compensation or an undertaking that the domestic law or procedure which gave rise to the complaint will be changed. The

Commission contacted the parties to see whether there was a possibility of a friendly settlement and passed on written proposals by the parties. The procedure was conducted in confidence and no details were made public.

Where no friendly settlement was achieved, the Commission would prepare a report on the merits, and lodge the case with the Committee of Ministers. The Commission's report would contain:
- a statement on admissibility;
- findings of facts; and
- an opinion on the alleged breach of the Convention.

The Committee of Ministers then had a maximum of three months during which either the government complained against or the Committee of Ministers would refer the case to the Court for a judgment.

The Court usually accepted the findings of facts made by the Commission. It independently examined the issues involved and the merits of the case. It invited written submissions prior to a hearing. Thus the advocate's role was reduced. Once the arguments were before the Court, the Court decided whether there had in fact been a violation of Convention right(s). The matter of enforcement was handed back to the Committee of Ministers. This procedure has now been amended pursuant to Protocol 11 (see below).

Diagrams 1 and 2 depict the old Strasbourg institutions and the old procedures respectively. These diagrams should be considered in conjunction with the detailed section on admissibility at page 30 *et seq.*

Diagram 1: The Old Institutions
Assuming:
- domestic remedies exhausted;
- complaint lodged within six months;
- complaint made by a victim:

Diagram 2: The Old Procedure

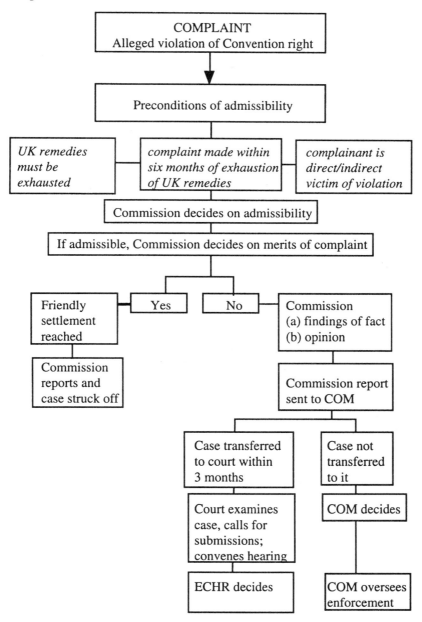

The New ECHR Structure

Protocol 11 to the Convention, which came into force in November 1998, created, effectively, a new and permanent Court of Human Rights, which replaced the Commission of Human Rights, although the Commission retained a "transitional role" until the end of October of 1999. The decision-making role of the Committee of Ministers in relation to Convention law has been removed.

The Court is based in Strasbourg, and comprises a Plenary Court, Chambers and the Grand Chambers (see below).

The Court's role is to receive complaints, decide on issues of admissibility and decide whether a complaint in fact amounts to a violation of a Convention right. In certain circumstances "Chamber" decisions can be appealed to a "Grand Chamber" – as to which see later. The Court, having decided that a Convention right has been violated, can order the state in question to pay appropriate compensation and costs to the aggrieved (Article 41).

Prior to November 1999, the Court was assisted by the opinions and interpretations given in Commission reports (above), although it was always the Court that decided whether and what amounted to a violation of a Convention right. There were many instances where the Court rejected the interpretations and opinions of the Commission, although their reports were, nonetheless, of great value.

The Court is empowered to give interpretations of its judgments if they are unclear, revise them if fresh evidence comes to light, and give advisory opinions to the Committee of Ministers.

Under Article 26 the Plenary Court is required to draw up the rules of procedure. The current rules were approved by the new court on taking up its duties in November 1998. The rules are provisional in the sense that they are bound to change in a number of respects as the Court gains experience in the workings of the new procedures. The Court can also hand down "Practice Directions" (Rule 32).

The primary responsibility for the administration of the work of the Court rests with the President and Vice President of the Court. These two are elected every three years by the judges from amongst their number (Rule 8).

The Parliamentary Assembly of the Council of Europe elects the judges from lists of three nominees put forward by each member state. Thus there are forty judges of the Court. Judges sit in their individual capacity. Generally, they hold office for a period of six years after which they must be re-elected. They must retire at the age of 70.

Article 23 sets out the general terms of the office. Judges are required to make a declaration of impartiality (Rule 2).

The full Court of forty judges does not usually sit in plenary session. Generally, the business of the Court is discharged in committees of three judges, Chambers of seven judges and occasionally by a Grand Chamber of seventeen judges.

The Plenary Court

The role of the Plenary Court is primarily one of administration. It does not therefore sit in a judicial capacity. By Article 26, the Plenary Court in a plenary session is required to:

* appoint a President and Vice President;
* set up Chambers;
* elect the President of the Chambers of the Court;
* adopt the Rules of the Court;
* elect the Registrars and Deputy Registrars.

Chambers

By Rule 49:

(a) All petitions and complaints are received by a judge known as a *rapporteur*. He or she decides whether the application should be referred to a Committee or to a Chamber of the Court. A Committee comprises three judges, and a Chamber, seven judges. A procedure exists for the consolidation of similar petitions.

(b) The Plenary Court sets up at least four Chambers and elects the President of each Chamber. As noted above, each Chamber consists of seven judges. The aim is to establish an equitable geographical composition of each Chamber, taking into account the different legal systems of the member states. There is likely to be sitting a judge from the jurisdiction in which the complaint originated. Rule 25(4) allows the President of each Chamber to make special arrangements concerning the constitution of the Chamber as he sees fit.

When a case is referred to a Committee, the Committee may decide that the petition in question is inadmissible and strike it out on a unanimous vote where such a decision can be made without further inquiry. Such a decision is final and no appeal lies (Article 28). Where the *rapporteur* has referred a petition to the Chambers, the Chamber will decide on admissibility and the merits of the petition. Generally, the decisions on admissibility and on the merits are taken separately

(Article 29). Where the petition is under Article 33 (inter-state petitions), admissibility is decided by a Chamber.

The Chamber establishes the facts in the case. It may, on its own motion or on submission from a party, call for or hear evidence if necessary and appropriate. The Chamber may also send a team or committee to seek out facts. It did so in, for example, *A v UK* [1980] 20 DR 5, where the conditions in Broadmoor were being examined, and in *Akdivar v Turkey* [1997] 23 EHRR 143, where an investigation into an allegation of the destruction of a village was required.

The decision to admit a petition is notified to the relevant member state and written submissions and observations invited. The Chamber holds a formal hearing. The old Commission imposed a strict time limit on the length of the oral submissions by each party. Under the new Rules of the Court pleadings and hearings are in public, although there are exceptions (Article 40). Like the Committee decision on admissibility, there is no appeal against an admissibility decision of the Chambers.

Under Article 42, Chambers judgments are final when the parties have indicated that they will not be requesting the Grand Chamber to hear an appeal; when three months have elapsed since the judgment of the Chamber; or when the Grand Chamber has rejected a request for an appeal (Article 44).

Under Article 30, a Chamber can relinquish jurisdiction in a case which raises serious questions affecting the interpretation of the Convention or the Protocol thereto, or where a Chamber decision might have a result which is inconsistent with a previous judgment delivered by the Court. In such instances jurisdiction goes to the Grand Chamber unless one of the parties to the case objects.

The Grand Chamber
The Grand Chamber consists of seventeen judges and three substitute judges. It has two distinct roles:
• To determine complex cases (Article 30) where a Chamber's case involves serious questions of interpretation of the Convention or where a Chamber decision may be inconsistent with a previous court decision (see above).
• To act as an appeal court. Under Article 43 a party may, within three months of a Chamber decision, ask that the case be referred to the Grand Chamber. This request is screened by a panel of five judges who may refer the case on to the Grand Chamber. The

Grand Chamber consists of the President and Vice President of the Court, the President of each Chamber and other judges appointed to reflect the various legal systems. A judge appointed by the respondent state also normally sits in the Grand Chamber. If not already a member of the Grand Chamber, he or she will sit in an *ex officio* capacity, taking the place of one of the judges. The appeals screening function of the Grand Chamber is carried out by five judges – the President and Vice President of the Court and three Presidents of Chambers (Rule 24).
Under Article 44, the judgment of the Grand Chamber is final.

The Registry
The Court's administrative work is carried out by its Registry, which comprises a number of lawyers who are supported by legal assistants and other back-up staff. The head of the Registry is the Registrar, who is a lawyer appointed by the Plenary Court. The Registrar's functions include:
- to assist the Court in the performance of its functions;
- to be responsible for the organisation and activities of the Registry;
- to provide the point of contact with the Court in relation to the cases brought.
- to prepare general instructions (sanctioned by the President) which govern the working procedure of the Registry.

Each Chamber has its own Registrar who has the day to day responsibility for the legal and administrative decisions of the Chamber.

The Committee of Ministers
The Committee of Ministers pre-dates the Convention, being a creature of the original Statute of the Council of Europe 1949. The Foreign Ministers of each member state of the Council of Europe make up the Committee. This is a political body and its main functions relate to the supervision of the Council of Europe's non-Convention business (the promotion of international treaties). This Committee had a substantial role in the Convention process, but much of it was abolished by Protocol 11. It does, however, retain one important Convention function. Under Article 46, the final judgment of the Court is sent to the Committee, one of whose functions is to ensure compliance by the member state concerned.

Diagrams 3A and 3B depict the new procedure under Protocol

11. These diagrams should be considered in conjunction with the de-tailed information on admissibility in Chapter 3. Although the struc-tures have changed, the admissibility criteria still apply and are unaf-fected by Protocol 11.

Diagram 3A: The New Structure

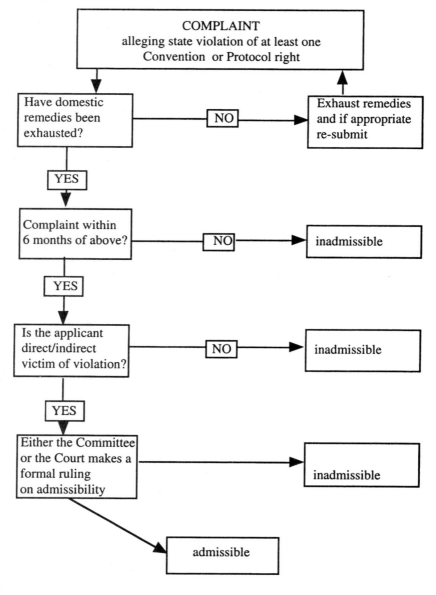

Diagram 3B: The New Procedure

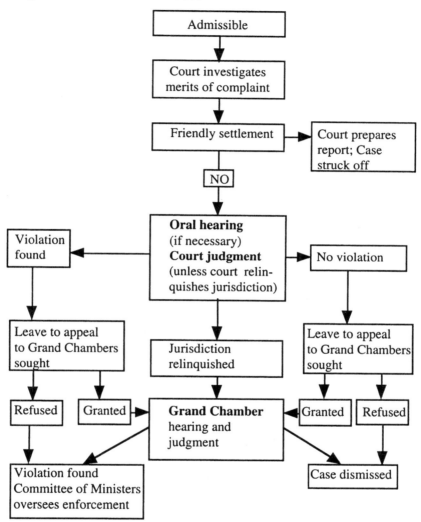

Checklist

The Old Strasbourg Structure
- The Commission.
- The Court.
- The Committee of Ministers.
- The greater role of the Committee of Ministers.
- Admissibility criteria:
  - exhaustion of domestic remedies,
  - six months time limit,
  - victim test to be satisfied.
- Friendly settlement was a feature of the process.
- Diagrams 1 and 2.

The New Strasbourg Structure
- Protocol 11 in force since November 1998.
- The new, permanent Court of Human Rights with its own administrative structure and rules.
- The Commission retained a transitional role which came to an end in October 1999.
- The decision-making role of the Committee of Ministers has been removed.
- Retention of the admissibility criteria – Article 35 and the jurisprudence under it.
- Petitions now received by the *rapporteur* who decides whether the petition should be referred to a Committee or the Chambers of the Court.
- Either of these rules on admissibility, although the admissibility on an inter-state petition under Article 33 is decided by a Chambers.
- Decisions on admissibility are final.
- Friendly settlement part of the process is retained.
- An appeal lies against a substantive judgment of the Chambers to the Grand Chamber.
- Diagrams 3A and 3B.

Chapter 3

The Complaints Procedure

Introduction

Protocol 11 establishes the complaints procedure. It creates for the first time in the history of international law a right for individuals to make member states accountable in an international court – the Court of Human Rights at Strasbourg – for alleged breaches of the Convention. No other international procedure allows or permits individuals to have direct access to an international court with the power to deliver judgments which are binding in international law.

The right of individual petition, under Article 34, is now a mandatory part of the Convention, although the jurisdiction of the court is limited. Petitions and complaints can be considered only if the admissibility criteria are met. These are set out in Article 35.1 which states:

> "The Court may only deal with the matter after all domestic remedies have been exhausted, according to the generally recognised rules of international law, and within six months from the date on which the final decision was taken . . ."

The following principles emerge from Article 35 and the jurisprudence under it:

- The complaint should be made by a victim (Article 34) or a potential victim.
- The complaint should engage a Convention issue – the matter complained of must be covered by the Convention and accepted by the member state.
- The alleged breach must have taken place at a time when the member state was bound by the Convention.
- The alleged breach must have taken place in the jurisdiction of the member state.
- All domestic remedies have to be exhausted.

- The alleged breach must have been raised in the domestic court.
- The complaint should be made within the six months of domestic remedies being exhausted.

Article 34 states:

> "The Court may receive applications from any person, non-governmental organisation or group of individuals claiming to be the victim of a violation. . . The High Contracting Parties undertake not to hinder in any way the effective exercise of this right."

This article requires states to allow individuals to bring complaints. It also obliges states not to hinder in any way the effective exercise of this right: *Akdivar v Turkey* [1997] 23 EHRR 143.

These preconditions for bringing a case to the Court of Human Rights are examined in more detail below.

The Complaint

The Complainant

Article 34 envisages applications from persons, including children and other incapacitated persons, whether or not represented by their parents, groups of individuals, companies, non-governmental organisations, political parties or churches. Petitioners need not be citizens of the state concerned, nor of any state of the Council of Europe. They do not have to be resident or physically present in the territory where the alleged breach took place, and they need not have been lawfully present there: *D v UK* [1997] 24 EHRR 423. Petitioners can seek anonymity but have to make their names known to the respondent state. A local government body or other "emanation of state" cannot be petitioners.

Group Complaint

Group complaints may be made by non-governmental organisations and groups of persons, excluding local governments. Politicians in their personal capacities and political parties can be complainants. However, groups of individuals or organisations cannot be petitioners simply because they wish to challenge a government action as a matter of principle. Concerned parties who are not themselves the victims cannot found an action. The Convention does not recognise "popular actions" or allow them to be brought. There must be a direct, indirect or potential victim.

Children

Children can take complaints themselves or through a guardian, official solicitor, lawyer or other representative. The court will require evidence of the person's authority to act for the child. Strasbourg recognises the vulnerability of children and that they have to rely on other persons to present their claims and represent their interests.

Death of victim

The next-of-kin may complain on behalf of a deceased victim: *Mc-Cann v UK* [1995] 21 EHRR 97 (the "death on the Rock" case). If the victim dies during the proceedings, the heir or other person(s) who can show a specific material interest in the complaint (or that it is of general interest) can carry on with the proceedings. Such persons may be parents, children, spouses or other close relatives.

Companies

Companies can found actions. Petitions can also be lodged by minority shareholders whom the domestic court recognises as having legal standing.

Victims

Article 34 requires that the petitioner must claim "to be a victim of a violation" of a Convention right. This article does not provide an exhaustive definition of such a victim, and it is therefore necessary to examine the relevant jurisprudence. Victims are actual, potential or indirect.

Actual Victim

An actual victim is somebody who has been personally affected by the alleged violation. He or she need not show that a detriment has been suffered, although that may be relevant to the question of "just satisfaction" under Article 41 (see page 44).

Potential Victim

A potential victim is someone who is at risk of being directly affected by a law or administrative act. The obvious examples are those under threat of expulsion by immigration authorities where the threat has not been carried out. Legislation permitting corporal punishment of a child who has not actually been so punished (*Campbell and Cosans v*

UK [1982] 4 EHRR 293) provides an example of potential victims. The mere possibility that corporal punishment may be inflicted can create potential victims. Another example of laws creating potential victims for the purposes of the Convention is the prohibition on homosexual acts between consenting adults, as in *Norris*, below. The concept of the potential victim is important in that it is new to common law lawyers.

In *Norris v Ireland* [1998] 13 EHRR 186 it was held that the mere existence of laws prohibiting homosexual acts between consenting adults made the complainants victims, even though the individuals were not prosecuted and it was made clear that the law would not be used. The court stated: "A law which remains on the statute book, even though it is not enforced . . . for a considerable time, may be applied again".

In *Malone v UK* [1984] 7 EHRR 14 (a telephone tapping case), the fact that the applicant was unable to establish that his telephone had been tapped was not a bar to his being held to be a victim.

Indirect Victim
Indirect victims are persons who are immediately affected by direct violations against others. Family members affected by the imprisonment, deportation or death of another may be indirect victims.

Respondents
Only those states that are party to the Convention can be brought to account for actual or potential violations. Complaints must, therefore, be directed at states which are parties to the Convention.

Where acts are carried out on behalf of states, the Convention responsibility cannot be passed on. For example, the state cannot absolve itself of responsibility for corporal punishment administered by institutions such as education authorities. A government cannot delegate responsibility and then seek to be absolved from that responsibility.

Complaints cannot be brought against private individuals. The court has said repeatedly that it is not "a court of fourth instance". It cannot act as a court of appeal from the decisions of national courts. It is said that the Convention has a "vertical" as opposed to a "horizontal" effect. This means, simply, that the Convention rights are actionable as between individuals and the states that govern those individuals.

The Subject of the Complaint

A Convention Issue

The complaint must be about a Convention issue. What is complained of should be covered by the Convention or any Protocol thereto, and the member state must have accepted that right. Convention rights accepted by the UK can be found in Part I of Schedule 1 to the Human Rights Act 1998. The court can examine complaints only if they relate to the rights and freedoms contained in the Convention. Not all member states of the Council of Europe have ratified all the protocols to the Convention. Complaints cannot be brought in relation to protocols and articles which a state has not ratified (see pages 141–142, on derogations and reservations, for the UK position).

Since Protocol 11, governments are no longer able to exclude from the right of individual petition complaints relating to any protocol which they may have ratified. Prior to Protocol 11, a state which had ratified a particular protocol was allowed not to accept a right of individual petition in relation to that particular protocol. Some states have entered derogations and reservations in respect of particular Convention articles and protocols, and are bound by them only to the extent that those states accept them.

Many "rights" issues are outside the Convention. There is no right to divorce, for example: *Johnston v Ireland* [1986] 9 EHRR 203. There is no right to a particular nationality. Nor is there a right to diplomatic protection, or to use the language of one's choice in dealing with any authority. Although some rights may seem to be outside the Convention – for example, there is no right to refugee status, no right to social security and no right to work – they may still be indirectly protected in some other way by other Convention or protocol provisions. Asylum seekers, for example, may be protected by the prohibition on torture or inhuman or degrading treatment, which includes the prohibition on expulsion to face the risk of such treatment: *Vilvarajah v UK* [1991] 14 EHRR 248.

The court cannot adjudicate on matters which are entirely outside the scope of the Convention.

Time at which the Alleged Violation Took Place

The criterion to be met under this heading is whether the alleged violation took place at a time when the member state in question was bound by the Convention. The court can examine complaints only if they allege that the state has violated its obligations under the Convention. Governments and states can be held responsible for violations only if they occur after they have accepted those obligations, i.e. after ratification and acceptance by the government or state of the right of individual petition and the subject to the terms of that acceptance. The UK accepted the right of individual petition in 1966. Since 1 November 1998 (the effective date for the commencement of Protocol 11) the right of individual petition has ceased to be optional. All states are answerable before the court for all alleged breaches which occur after that date. It is therefore important to determine whether or not the government or state had ratified the Convention and had accepted the right of individual petition when the alleged violation of the Convention took place.

Place at Which Violation Took Place

A state can be liable only for violations that take place in its jurisdiction. All violations which take place in a state's territory will normally be in that state's jurisdiction, but this does not mean that violations which take place outside a particular state's territory are necessarily outside its jurisdiction. The crucial question is whether or not the state was exercising effective control over the events in question. In a case against Turkey the court held that Turkey could exercise effective control over an area in Northern Cyprus and therefore could be responsible for violations which occurred there despite the fact that it was outside Turkey's national territory. The court upheld this as a matter of principle, stating that "whether the control was exercised by the state directly, or through its armed forces or through a subordinate local administration" was to be considered.

Another example of a violation which takes place outside the territory of a member state, but where that state's responsibility may still be engaged, is where that government extradites or expels a person to face the risk of prohibited treatment: *Chahal v UK* [1996] 23 EHRR 413. The sending state's responsibilities come into play whether or not, for example, Article 3 (prohibition on torture) arises in the country of destination, because of the direct actions of a state or the direct actions of private individuals or simply by the social conditions that exist in the state of destination.

The Commission has also considered the issue of whether a government will be responsible where it expels an individual who faces detention and trial which would be a "flagrant denial of justice". It is possible that some petitions can be based on the fact that if a government expels or extradites an individual he or she will not receive a fair trial, guaranteed by Article 6, in the country of destination. That remains to be seen.

Exhaustion of Domestic Remedies

The exhaustion of domestic remedies is one of the most important procedural aspects of the Convention. Many petitions fail because the petitioner/applicant or the lawyers have underestimated the significance of this requirement. Under Article 1 of the Convention, governments are under an obligation to "secure" the rights and freedoms in the Convention to its citizens within its jurisdiction. This obligation requires each government to put in place a legal framework to allow its citizens to secure those rights and freedoms. In addition to the Article 1 requirement, Article 13 requires member states to make available in their national jurisdictions "effective remedies" for violations of Convention rights. The UK has not incorporated Article 13; see page 142.

In *Handyside v UK* [1976] 1 EHRR 737 it was said:

" . . . The Convention leaves to each Contracting State, in the first place, the task of securing the rights and freedoms it enshrines. The institutions created by it make their own contribution to this task but they become involved only through contentious proceedings and once all domestic remedies have been exhausted."

The underlying principle is that the primary responsibility for securing the rights and freedoms under the Convention lies with the governments and their own institutions. The Human Rights Court steps in when that protection has failed. Therefore, no petition or complaint can be made unless it can be shown that the relevant government and its institutions have failed in this respect. Unless all domestic remedies have been tried and failed, it will not be possible to show that the government is in violation of the Convention rights. Petitioners are required to provide the national court with the opportunity of preventing or putting right violations alleged against them: *Cardot v France* [1991] 13 EHRR 853. The Human Rights Court is therefore in addition to the national systems of member states.

There is a also a general rule in international law that recourse may not be had to international tribunals until every domestic or national remedy has been tried and failed. The international court may deal with the matter only after all domestic remedies have been exhausted. This is to ensure that the government has been given the opportunity to resolve the matter nationally by placing it before the national court to test the alleged breach in the normal way. Such requirements also minimise the case-loads of international fora, including the Human Rights Court.

If the Human Rights Court rejects a petition on the ground of failure to exhaust domestic remedies, the petition can be re-submitted when domestic remedies have been pursued and exhausted. If a national domestic remedy is no longer available, as where, for example, the applicant is out of time according to national rules, then the matter is at an end, unless the applicant can pursue the case in the Human Rights Court.

The requirement to exhaust all domestic remedies is applied strictly.

The right to a remedy does not imply the right to a decision in favour of the victim/petitioner. There may be instances where a victim fails to establish a right of access; or, having established a right of access, fails to prove entitlement to the remedy on the merits of the case. The distinction is subtle but the consequences may be quite serious. Firstly, the victim may not even begin to have the complaint heard because it falls into a category which cannot be justiciable. Secondly, the victim, having had the complaint heard because it falls into a category which can be justiciable, fails to obtain a favourable judgment. In *Osman v UK* [1988] Application No 00023452/94, *The Times*, 5 November 1998, [1999] EHRLR 228 (see page 77), the case was rejected on the basis that the domestic law in question did not allow, as a matter of public policy, actions against the police for alleged negligent police investigations. The victim was denied access to a remedy, as opposed to not being entitled to a remedy on the merits of the claim. It is therefore important to distinguish between the right of access to a remedy, and entitlement to a remedy on the merits of the case.

The Onus of Proof

The application to the court requires the applicant to set out the steps taken to exhaust the available domestic remedies. Once the applicant submits that all such remedies have been exhausted, it is for the government in question, if it is taking the point, to demonstrate that the applicant did not make use of a remedy that was available in a domestic court. The onus is on the government not only to show that there was an effective domestic remedy which the applicant failed to pursue, but that the applicant had access to that remedy.

The government must also indicate in clear terms, if it takes the point, those remedies to which the applicant has not had recourse. If the court is satisfied of the availability of national domestic remedies which the petitioner has not used, the burden of proving that those remedies were ineffective rests with the petitioner/applicant. If the government fails to raise this point at the admissibility stage, it may be estopped from relying on it at the final merits hearing.

If a government, during the proceedings in the national domestic courts, argues that a particular national domestic remedy is not available to the petitioner, the government will not be allowed to argue before the Human Rights Court that the remedy was in fact available. In other words, the government will not be allowed to change its stance at the hearing before the Human Rights Court.

Deemed Exhaustion
If there is no prospect of an appeal or other judicial remedy being successful in the domestic courts, then such a course need not necessarily be pursued as a prerequisite of a petition to the Court of Human Rights. Often there simply is no domestic remedy available. As we have seen, the permissibility of corporal punishment and the laws prohibiting consensual homosexual activity between adults in private are instances where no domestic remedy is available. In point of fact such a situation is a "continuing violation" of Convention rights – as in *Norris* above.

Generally speaking, the Court of Human Rights will accept the opinion of a senior lawyer of the state in question, experienced in the field, on the question of exhaustion of domestic remedies. Governments tend to assert non-exhaustion as a matter of course unless the proceedings have been through the whole appeal process in the domestic courts. Where the Court of Human Rights is provided with a junior lawyer's opinion on the chances of success of an appeal in the domestic courts, the government in question sometimes argues that the opinion of a senior lawyer should have been obtained.

In practice the Court of Human Rights is shown a copy of the lawyer's opinion on the exhaustion of domestic remedies or the unlikelihood that domestic proceedings would succeed, and the possibility of this should be kept in mind by lawyers called upon to advise. Any advice or opinion, in due course, might be copied to the Court of Human Rights and to the government complained of. If an advice or opinion is unfavourable it should explain in detail why the proposed appeal or other course of action would be ineffective, for example, by referring to the approach taken by the government or the national courts on a Convention right. Lawyers should also bear in mind that their advice and opinions may be published. Obviously, where there is a long line of decided cases showing that a further appeal is bound to fail then there may be no need for the court to have a senior lawyer's opinion.

Sometimes the court will allow "special circumstances" on non-exhaustion of domestic remedies by the applicant. The applicant could claim that the availability of national domestic remedies would be ineffective in practice because, for example, the strict application of the exhaustion rule would unfairly and unreasonably subject the applicant to further violation of his rights (such as mistreatment in prison).

If domestic remedies fail because incorrect procedures have been adopted, as a result of a mistake by the applicant or his representatives, then domestic remedies are said not to have been exhausted. If, for example, an action is started in the High Court by way of claim in circumstances when judicial review was the appropriate procedure, by the time the applicant pursues the judicial review procedure, it may be that the petition is out of time. The petitioner runs the risk, in these circumstances, of having his or her petition rejected, since it is likely that Strasbourg will rule such a petition inadmissible on the ground of non-exhaustion.

Effective Remedies

The available domestic remedies have to be effective. Although Article 13 does not require that the remedies be judicial remedies for them to be effective, some non-judicial remedies have been held to be ineffective for the purposes of the exhaustion rule, while others have, in certain circumstances, been found effective. The Court of Human Rights has not accepted the effectiveness of certain remedies when the government complained of has alleged non-exhaustion. There are clearly certain procedures which cannot amount to an "effective remedy". Examples are royal pardons and *ex gratia* payments. Discretionary remedies may not be effective remedies. However, the fact that a remedy is in certain respects discretionary does not necessarily make it an ineffective remedy. In *Reid v UK* [1983] 5 EHRR 114 a prisoner had complained about his solitary confinement and challenged it by petitioning the Home Office and the Board of Visitors. The Court of Human Rights held that the applicant had exhausted his domestic remedies. In general, however, a remedy which depends upon the discretionary power of a public authority cannot be considered to be effective. The Ombudsman procedure is generally thought not to be an effective remedy. An appeal from a tribunal where the appeal is limited to questions of law is not an effective remedy where the complaint relates to facts as well as law, particularly if the complaint is about *quantum* of compensation and the size of the damages is determined by formula laid down in statute: *Lithgow v UK* [1986] 8 EHRR 329.

Whether the judicial review procedure is an effective remedy depends on the circumstances of the individual case. There has been a series of cases largely concerned with immigration, asylum and extradition where the judicial review procedure has been found wanting.

Where there is a choice of remedies open to the complainant, the court only expects the obvious and sensible one to be pursued. It accepts that the rule of exhaustion of domestic remedies can be applied only to reflect the practical realities of the individual's position. On the other hand, an applicant cannot ignore a remedy that is generally held to be available and effective. Therefore, the burden of choosing the appropriate and correct remedy is considerable. If a number of potentially effective remedies exist, the applicant will be required to pursue them. The case of *Chappell v UK* [1990] 12 EHRR 1 concerned an *Anton Piller* search; the complainant alleged that the documents seized went beyond the scope of the litigation in question. The Court of Human Rights agreed that in those circumstances the following remedies existed: application on the basis of contempt of court; application for damages from the third party who obtained the order; and an application to the court for the return of the documents.

It follows from the rule that domestic remedies have to be exhausted before it can be alleged that a state has failed in its obligations under Article 1 to secure for the applicant one or more of his Convention rights, that the Convention rights and freedoms in issue must have been raised in the domestic proceedings. The issue which the petitioner complains of needs to have been considered by the domestic courts.

The Six Month Time Limit

Article 35 stipulates that the Court of Human Rights may only deal with the matter within a period of six months from the date on which the final decision in the domestic proceedings was taken. The court applies the time limit strictly on the basis that the purpose of the rule was to ensure a degree of legal certainty and to ensure that cases raising problems under the Convention are examined within a reasonable time. The rule is also intended to prevent authorities and other persons concerned from being in a state of uncertainty for a prolonged period. Lastly, the rule is designed to facilitate the establishment of the facts of the case which, with the passage of time, would otherwise become increasingly difficult.

Relevant Date

The six months run from the moment the applicant is aware of the matter of the complaint and has exhausted all (if any) effective domestic remedies. In practice this is the time when he or she is told of the outcome, either by being present when the decision is made, or if precluded from being present, by being told by his or her lawyer. Sometimes judgments are not pronounced in open court, in which case the six months time limit may run from the time the judgment is served. It also often happens that, although the lawyers and those that they represent are present when the judgment is handed down, the judgment is not available in written form until some time afterwards. In that case the relevant time for the purpose of this rule is the date on which the written text is served. In *Isabel Hilton v UK* [1988] 57 DR 108 the petitioner was refused a job with the BBC. Nine years later she discovered that the refusal might have arisen from a secret M15 vetting process. Here the court held that the six month period was to run from the time the petitioner discovered this fact.

It is submitted that the issue of when the six months time limit begins and ends is somewhat complex, and practitioners should be aware of the difficulties in pinpointing the exact starting date. The message seems to be to know the domestic procedure well and opt for the correct remedy; not to be defeated by domestic time limits; and to ascertain the effective date for the purpose of the six month time limit. Time runs from the exhaustion of the last effective remedy, and not from the failure of later proceedings for an ineffective remedy.

Frequently a petitioner may have to wait some time before knowing whether there is an effective appeal (or other domestic remedy) and then may have to wait to see if leave is granted or the case reopened. It may be that, by the time a remedy has been shown to be ineffective, the six months period has expired. To deal with such a problem and if the applicant is in doubt as to the effective date for the purposes of the rule, an application should be submitted to the Court of Human Rights as well as pursuing the domestic appeal. If the appeal is found to be an effective remedy, it will be possible to re-submit the application to the Court of Human Rights, if then necessary. If ineffective, the application will be in time. Sometimes a potential complaint lies in respect of more than one breach of the Convention, as where the domestic remedy is exhausted in respect of one aspect but not others. Again it would be sensible to submit a complaint to the Court of Human Rights setting out the claim in full and pointing out that in respect of certain matters domestic remedies are still being pursued.

The End of the Six Months
The final date in determining whether the application is within six months is the date of the first letter, telex or fax to the court – provided it contains basic details of the nature of the complaint. The mere submission of documents is not enough; the complaint must be raised in express or implied form.

In a continuing situation – as where there is no domestic remedy because a particular law exists (prohibition of homosexual acts – *Norris v Ireland*, above) the six months time limit does not apply.

The original complaint must deal with the full details of the alleged violation(s). A failure to detail the precise nature and extent of the complaint may be rejected as out of time. In *B v UK* DR 45/41, the applicant complained of civil service disciplinary proceedings arising out of a press comment he had made in connection with his employment at Aldermaston Atomic Research Centre. Subsequent to his original application, in correspondence, he raised a complaint about violations of other articles arising out of the same incident. The court held that these new matters were out of time and therefore inadmissible. It is a matter of construction whether subsequent clarification of the original complaint is merely clarification, or whether it amounts to a fresh complaint. The alleged violations should, therefore, be set out in full in the original complaint.

The Court of Human Rights does, however, sometimes accept delay if there are compelling reasons.

Inadmissibility

One of the court's primary functions is to sift through the large number of applications and exclude the hopeless. Some applications do not come within the scope of the Convention at all, or the facts alleged could never amount to violations.

In addition to the above detailed grounds for rejecting applications, Article 35.2 sets out further grounds. Thus, the court will not deal with any application that is:

• anonymous, or
• substantially the same as a matter which has been examined by the court or has already been submitted to another procedure of international investigation or settlement or contains no relevant new information.

Article 35.3 provides that the court shall consider inadmissible any petition which it considers incompatible with the provisions of the Convention or the Protocols thereto, manifestly ill-founded or an abuse of the right of application.

Although anonymous complaints are inadmissible, a petitioner can request that his or her identity is not disclosed.

The rules on matters which are substantially the same as others is to prevent applicants from submitting repeat applications on substantially the same facts. Where new facts emerge, however, a repeat application may be allowed. Where an application is rejected because of non-exhaustion of domestic remedy another application will be allowed after the domestic remedies have been exhausted – the new facts being the exhaustion of domestic remedies.

Examination by another international body includes referrals to, for example, the United Nations Human Rights Committee, although the UK has not signed the protocol which would enable an individual to lodge complaints with the Committee. It remains to be seen whether proceedings before the Court of Justice of the European Communities at Luxembourg constitute an "international investigation".

"Incompatible with the provisions of the Convention" includes complaints which are outside the scope of the Convention, complaints against non-members and complaints not directed against states. All these are examples of petitions which are bound to fail. Sometimes petitions allege breaches of rights and freedoms not protected by the Convention, such as the right to work and the right to nature conservation. Again, these are inadmissible.

Applications which are "manifestly ill-founded" include those which, on a preliminary examination, do not disclose any possible ground upon which it can be alleged that the Convention has been violated; for example, complaints based on facts which are demonstrably wrong or incapable of substantiation.

Although applications will be deemed inadmissible if they constitute an abuse of the right of petition, a desire to embarrass a state is not in itself a bar to admissibility. Nor is the fact that a petitioner does not come to the court "with clean hands" necessarily a bar to admissibility.

If the applicant relies on obviously untrue evidence or facts, or if the application is vexatious (bearing in mind previous applications), the application is likely to be rejected as inadmissible.

Friendly Settlement

Article 38.1.b states:

> "If the Court declares the application admissible, it shall . . . place itself at the disposal of the parties concerned with a view to securing a friendly settlement of the matter on the basis of respect for human rights as defined in the Convention and the protocols thereto".

Proceedings conducted under paragraph 1.b are confidential. Once the petition has been declared admissible, the Registrar of the court inquires with the parties whether a friendly settlement is possible. The court will have to verify any such settlement, and a report on the settlement is sent to the Committee of Ministers, which will oversee enforcement of the terms of the settlement.

Under Article 39, if a friendly settlement is effected, the court strikes out the case. The decision will be confined to a brief statement of the facts and of the resolutions reached.

Just Satisfaction
Article 41 states:
> "If the Court finds that there has been a violation of the Convention or the protocols thereto, and if the internal law of the High Contracting Party concerned allows only partial reparation to be made, the Court shall, if necessary afford just satisfaction to the injured party."

Just satisfaction may include damages, compensation, costs and expenses. A claim for just satisfaction has to be specifically pleaded in the documents submitted to the court.

Costs and Expenses
The petitioner must prove that any costs claimed are costs actually incurred and that the petitioner is liable to pay them. Expenses may also be claimed. In *Sunday Times v UK* [1979] 2 EHRR 245 the court recognised that not awarding costs could be seen as a hindrance to the effective protection of human rights.

No fees are payable to the court and there is no requirement to meet the costs incurred by a member state (the respondent).

Legal Aid
Under the rules governing the Court of Human Rights there is a system for the provision of legal aid by that court. It seems likely, and indeed desirable, that where human rights violations are alleged and a complainant wishes to pursue that allegation in the domestic court, the UK Legal Services Commission will grant legal aid. However, legal aid from Strasbourg is available from the point when the petition has been communicated to the member state. Contingency fees are recognised by Strasbourg. The Court of Human Rights, upon receipt of a petitioner's application for legal aid, sends a copy to the respondent member state for its observations and comments. Strasbourg will subject the application to a means test. The court may, however, deduct an amount from any damages received by the petitioner. See Chapter X of the Rules of the European Court of Human Rights.

Binding Force and Execution of Judgments

Under Article 46:

> "1 The High Contracting Parties undertake to abide by the final judgment of the Court in any case to which they are parties.
>
> 2 The final judgment of the Court shall be transmitted to the Committee of Ministers, which shall supervise its execution."

The judgments of the Strasbourg court do not have the effect of overturning national decisions and domestic legislation is not invalidated. This is also the scheme adopted by the Human Rights Act 1998 (see pages 49–50).

Under Article 46, member states undertake to respect judgments from Strasbourg. The Committee of Ministers supervises the enforcement of the court's judgments. Failure on the part of member states to meet the terms or requirements of an adverse judgment may lead the Committee of Ministers to take measures, so long as there is a two-thirds majority in favour. The added sanction for non-compliance is the diplomatic, international and other pressure that may be brought to bear upon a member state, although in reality there may not be much that can be done to force compliance. The final step would be for the Committee of Ministers to invoke its powers to suspend or expel any member state from the Council of Europe for serious and persistent breaches of human rights. The UK has a strong record of taking steps to correct and meet the recommendations of the Committee of Ministers, on many occasions introducing legislation for the purpose. Examples are the Interception of Communications Act 1985 and the Special Immigration Appeals Commission Act 1998, both of which were passed following adverse Strasbourg judgments in the cases of *Malone v UK* [1984] 7 EHRR 14 and *Chahal v UK* [1996] 23 EHRR 413 respectively.

Checklist

- Protocol 11 establishes the new structure and complaints procedure.
- The right of individual petition is now a mandatory part of the Convention.
- Admissibility criteria – Article 35 and its jurisprudence – retained.
- Domestic remedies must be exhausted.
- Six months time limit on petitioning the Court of Human Rights.

- Admissibility criteria are the same as those that prevailed prior to Protocol 11.
- The petition must be brought by a person claiming to be a victim; Article 34 and the jurisprudence thereunder. The victim may be an actual, potential or indirect victim.
- Articles 1 and 13 requirements: it is a matter for national courts to make available in their jurisdictions the rights and remedies under the Convention, hence the requirement for exhaustion of domestic remedies as part of the admissibility criteria.
- The subject of the complaint. The complaint must be about a matter covered by the Convention and the right complained of must have been adopted by the government in question – see Schedule 1, Human Rights Act 1998.
- The onus on the practitioner is to thoroughly understand:
  - the admissibility criteria;
  - the procedure;
  - the relevant dates for the purpose of the six months time limit;
  - the domestic remedies.

Chapter 4

The Human Rights Act 1998

The General Scheme of the Act

In the Human Rights Act 1998 it is sought to promote a number of themes and ideas, based on constitutional and theoretical imperatives:

- the retention of parliamentary legislative supremacy;
- the rights and freedoms under the Convention and the Protocols as adopted by the Act; these appear in Sched 1 to the Act;
- the rights and freedoms under the Convention and the Protocols are not, however, given "entrenched" status;
- the Act is not a "full incorporation" of the Convention;
- the Convention and its jurisprudence and any adverse judgments of the Court of Human Rights are not binding in domestic law;
- the recognition that human rights and fundamental freedoms are not an entirely new idea to domestic courts;
- the Act makes available, in domestic courts, the Convention rights by meeting the requirements of Articles 1 and 13 through the "interpretative obligation" and by providing judicial remedies.

Parliamentary Legislative Supremacy

The principle of parliamentary legislative supremacy is the constitutional doctrine that there is nothing, so far as the domestic law is concerned, that a properly enacted statute cannot do. Parliament can make or unmake any law as it chooses. To this extent, Parliament is supreme. This elementary and basic rule of English constitutional law, on the face of it, leaves domestic courts with no option but to interpret and construe an Act of Parliament as it stands. We have seen in Chapter 1 that, for an international treaty or its provisions to become part of domestic law, Parliament must adopt or enact domestic legislation. It has been argued, rightly or wrongly, that parliamentary legislative supremacy was surrendered by the European Communities

Act 1972. This is not a criticism that can be levelled at the Human Rights Act 1998 for it jealously guards the principle, as we shall see.

Absence of Entrenchment

On one view (not adopted by the Act), human rights and fundamental freedoms are so important that they should be given added constitutional protection by elevating them to a status higher than the "ordinary" domestic law – the rights and freedoms embodied in the Convention should sit over and above other "ordinary" domestic law. Further, that to amend or repeal human rights and fundamental freedoms there has to be a special procedure. For example, under the American Constitution certain rights and freedoms are guaranteed and can be amended or repealed only by a qualified majority. The process of affording certain rights a higher status and the requirement for a special procedure to amend or repeal them is called "entrenchment".

Entrenchment is not a principle of the UK constitution. Indeed, entrenchment of any UK law could not be reconciled with the UK constitution, since its effect would be an attempt to tie the hands of future Parliaments. This would violate the principle of parliamentary legislative supremacy which allows any laws to be amended or repealed by a subsequent Act of Parliament. Indeed, The Government's White Paper (October 1997) explained: "We do not believe that it is necessary or would be desirable to attempt to devise such a special arrangement for this Bill".

The government thus rejected the notion that the Convention and the rights under it should have entrenched status in domestic law, adopting the prevailing legal philosophy that Parliament is supreme. This, it is submitted, is in accordance with the other key themes embodied in the Human Rights Act 1998.

Absence of Incorporation

Although the Convention rights are available in domestic courts from the coming into force of the Human Rights Act, such availability should not be equated with "full incorporation". The Convention and the rights under it are "incorporated" only to the extent that ss 2, 3 and 6 of the Human Rights Act 1998 (the "interpretative obligation", see page 53 *et seq*) allow.

The position adopted in the Human Rights Act is to be contrasted with the position taken in the European Communities Act 1972 which incorporated the Treaty of Rome and made it "part of our law" to the extent required by the principle of "direct effect". Broadly speaking, certain EC laws are directly effective in UK domestic law without the need for domestic legislation. The general application and the direct applicability of Regulations is fundamental to the scheme of the EEC. Under Article 189/249 of the EC Treaty:

". . . A regulation shall have general application. It shall be binding in its entirety and directly applicable in all Member States".

Section 2(1) of the European Communities Act 1972 provides:

"All such rights, powers, liabilities, obligations . . . are without further enactment to be given legal effect or used in the United Kingdom shall be recognised and available in law, and be enforced, allowed and followed accordingly . . . "

In Case 26/62 *Van Gend en Loos* [1963] ECR 1, the Court of Justice of the European Communities (CJEC) said that the member states of the EC have surrendered their sovereign rights, albeit within a limited sphere. This has been reiterated in several other cases.

In a number of cases the CJEC has held that as a matter of EC law some of the provisions of the EC Treaty confer rights which domestic courts must respect and give effect to, and that domestic law cannot prevail over EEC law, regardless of which was first in time. If the CJEC declares a piece of domestic legislation inconsistent with an EC law, the member state in question is under an obligation to amend or repeal the offending domestic legislation, and domestic courts are under a duty to comply with the judgments of the CJEC. Where EC law has "direct effect" in domestic law it takes precedence over domestic law.

Certain EC laws are "incorporated" into domestic law without further enactment, making those EC laws "part of our law". They are binding and take primacy over domestic law. It is a requirement of EC membership that member states give priority to directly effective EC laws in domestic law. The scheme of the European Communities Act 1972 is to give effect, without more, in domestic law to rights and duties under the EC Treaty which have direct effect.

Non-Binding Nature of Convention Jurisprudence
There is no requirement of direct effect under the Convention, which does not insist on assuming primacy over domestic law. The Convention jurisprudence is not binding on domestic courts and any adverse judgments of the Convention institutions are not binding. The scheme

of the Human Rights Act 1998 is not to give primacy to the Convention and its jurisprudence. Domestic law prevails until such time as the Westminster Parliament changes any offending and incompatible piece of domestic legislation.

The Lord Chancellor (Lord Irvine of Lairg), at the Report Stage of the passage of the Bill, explained (*Hansard,* HL, 19 January 1998, col 1270): " . . . the word 'binding' is the language of strict precedent but the Convention has no rule of precedent . . . ".

Because the Convention is a "living instrument" (see page 12), it follows that there cannot be a formal and rigid system of precedent as in the common law. The language used in ss 2, 3 and 6 of the Human Rights Act 1998 reflects this.

The Requirements of Articles 1 and 13
Another theme in the Act is to meet the requirements of Articles 1 and 13 of the Convention by making available the rights and remedies in domestic courts via ss 2, 3 and 6 (the interpretative obligation) and ss 7, 8 and 9 (on proceedings and judicial remedies).

The Act also recognises that the Convention rights and freedoms are not entirely new to the domestic system. We saw in Chapter 1 that, through a number of devices (such as presumptions of interpretation, minimum international standards and European Community law), such rights and freedoms were available in domestic courts – supported by the existing body of case law. In the past the Convention rights and freedoms were available only through "indirect" devices, but the Human Rights Act 1998 makes these rights and freedoms directly and formally available to a citizen in the domestic courts. It is perhaps to these indirect devices that the Lord Chancellor referred when he said (Reports Stage, *Hansard* HL, 29 January 1998, col 421):

> " . . . the word 'further' is included in the Long Title because, in our national arrangements the Convention can, and is, relied on in a range of ways by our own courts."

The Principal Provisions of the Act
As has been seen above, EC law imposes additional demands and requirements upon domestic systems, but no such demands are made or requirements imposed by the Convention and its jurisprudence, other than the requirements in Articles 1 and 13.

Article 1 of the Convention requires the member states to secure to everyone within their jurisdictions the rights and freedoms under the Convention.

Article 13 requires that everyone whose rights and freedoms under the Convention are violated shall have an effective remedy before a national authority.

It is not a requirement of the Convention that member states harmonise and equalise their domestic laws and procedures. It is therefore for each member state to ensure that the Convention rights are justiciable in its national courts. The Court of Human Rights becomes involved only after the national remedies and procedures have been exhausted and failed.

The Human Rights Act 1998 gives effect to Article 1 by securing to the citizens of the UK the rights and freedoms under the Convention. The Act sets out a scheme which gives effect to Convention rights, and which maximises the protection afforded, whilst retaining the principle of parliamentary legislative supremacy. It gives effect to Article 13 by establishing a scheme under which Convention rights can be raised and argued before the national courts, and s 8 of the Act provides for judicial remedies.

Thus the general scheme of the Act is to meet the requirements of Articles 1 and 13 through the "interpretative obligation" and by providing additional, substantive causes of actions and remedies.

In addition to meeting the requirements of Articles 1 and 13, the Act preserves, skilfully and ingeniously, the doctrine of parliamentary legislative supremacy in ss 3(2)(b), (c), 4(6) and 6(2).

The Lord Chancellor (Lord Irvine of Lairg) summed up the Act quite well when he said in the House of Lords Report Stage that the Act (then a Bill) does not make the Convention "part of our law". He explained (Reports Stage, *Hansard* HL, 29 January 1998, col 421):

"The bill will greatly increase the ability of our courts to enforce the Convention rights, but it is not introducing a wholly new concept. As I have said before, the Bill does not as such incorporate Convention rights into domestic law; in accordance with the language of the Long Title, it gives further effect in the UK to Convention rights by requiring the courts in [s 3(1)] to read and give effect to primary legislation and subordinate legislation in a way which is compatible with the Convention rights. That is an interpretative principle . . .

I have to make this point absolutely plain. The European

Convention of Human Rights under this [Act] is not made part of our law. The [Act] gives the European Convention of Human Rights a special relationship which will mean that the courts will give effect to the interpretative provisions to which I have already referred, but it does not make the Convention directly justiciable as it would be if it were expressly made part of our law. I want there to be no ambiguity about that . . .

The short point is that if the Convention rights were incorporated into our law they would be enforced by our courts. That is not the scheme of this Act. If the courts find it impossible to construe primary legislation in a way compatible with the Convention rights, the primary legislation remains in force and effect. All that the courts may do is to make a declaration of incompatibility."

The Convention Rights

Section 1(1) defines the Convention and Protocol rights adopted by the Act. For the purposes of the Act "the Convention rights" are those set out in Articles 1 to 12 and 14 of the Convention, Articles 1 to 3 of the First Protocol; and Articles 1 and 2 of the Sixth Protocol. Section 1(2) provides that the articles and rights under them are to have effect subject to any reservation or derogation (as to which see ss 14 and 15).

The Articles referred to in s 1 appear in Part I of Sched 1 to the Act (s 1(3)).

The Secretary of State is empowered to amend the Act as appropriate to reflect the effect of a Protocol (s 1(4)). The protocols referred to in subs 4 means those that have been ratified by the UK or which the UK government has signed with a view to ratification – see Parts II and III of Sched 1 to the Act (s 1(5)). Amendments under subs (4) may be effective only when the relevant protocol is in force.

Interpretation of Convention Rights

Under s 2(1), a court or tribunal dealing with a Convention issue which has arisen before it must take into account:
  • the judgments, decisions, declarations and advisory opinions of the Court of Human Rights;
  • the opinions of the Commission of Human Rights;

- the decisions of the Commission;
- the decisions of the Committee of Ministers.

(the above are referred to collectively as the "Strasbourg jurisprudence"), whenever made or given . . . (overlooking the doctrine of "implied repeal").

The court or tribunal will have to be satisfied that a Convention issue is relevant to the proceedings before it.

Evidence of the jurisprudence which is to be taken into account is to be given in such manner as may be prescribed by rules (s 2(2)).

"Rules" mean the rules of the court or other rules made pursuant to s 2 (e.g. tribunal rules) (s 2(3)).

Comment: In this section we see the beginnings of what has been referred to as the "interpretative obligation": the obligation is to *take into account* the Strasbourg jurisprudence. This section does not require a court or tribunal to follow or be bound by the Strasbourg jurisprudence.

The court or tribunal must take into account the Strasbourg jurisprudence whether or not it arose before or after the relevant domestic law. The "implied repeal" argument is thus swept to one side.

Interpretation of Legislation

Section 3(1) requires that, so far as it is possible to do so, primary and subordinate legislation must be read and given effect in a way which is compatible with the Convention rights. Section 3(1):

- applies to primary legislation and subordinate legislation whenever enacted;
- does not affect the validity, continuing operation or enforcement of any incompatible primary legislation; and
- does not affect the validity, continuing operation or enforcement of any incompatible subordinate legislation if (disregarding any possibility of revocation) primary legislation prevents the removal of the incompatibility.

Comment: This is a key section in the "interpretative obligation" and it is in this section that the concept solidifies. Unlike s 2 of the Act, this section is not aimed at any specific authority or person. It can therefore be said to impose an obligation on everyone – not just courts and tribunals – to interpret legislation compatibly with the

Convention. The use of the word "whenever" also sweeps to one side any arguments of implied repeal, as in relation to s 2 above. The requirement is for legislation to be interpreted, so far as it is possible to do so, compatibly with the Convention. If it is not possible to interpret primary domestic legislation compatibly, then the legislation in question remains valid and will continue to be applied and enforced. This is the practical effect of s 3(2)(b). This subsection retains the principle of parliamentary legislative supremacy, as mentioned earlier in this chapter.

Where a court is concerned with interpreting a piece of subordinate legislation which derives its authority from a parent Act of Parliament which prevents the removal of the incompatibility, then the practical effects will be the same as in respect of primary legislation, i.e. that the subordinate legislation remains valid and will continue to be applied and enforced. This is the practical effect of s 3(2)(c), which further retains the principle of parliamentary legislative supremacy.

The position may be different, however, where the court is concerned with interpreting a free-standing piece of subordinate legislation which does not derive its authority from a piece of primary legislation. Free-standing subordinate legislation may be invalidated or disapplied if incompatible with a Convention right.

Declarations of Incompatibility

If the court or tribunal arrives at a compatible interpretation and so is satisfied that the domestic legislation in question is compatible with the Convention rights, it proceeds in the normal way. If a compatible position cannot be arrived at, s 4 comes into play.

Section 4(2) applies in any proceedings in which a court is considering whether a provision of primary legislation is compatible with a Convention right (s 4(1)). It provides that if the court is satisfied that the provision is incompatible with a Convention right, it may make a "declaration of that incompatibility".

Subsection (4) applies in any proceedings in which a court is considering whether a provision of subordinate legislation, which has its roots in primary legislation, is compatible with a Convention right (s 4(3)). It provides that, if a court is satisfied:

• that the provision is incompatible with a Convention right, and
• that (disregarding any possibility of revocation) the relevant pri-

mary legislation prevents the removal of that incompatibility, it may make a declaration of that incompatibility.

Only certain courts, however, have the power to make such a declaration. They are:

- the House of Lords;
- the Judicial Committee of the Privy Council;
- the Courts-Martial Appeal Court;
- in Scotland, the High Court of Justiciary sitting otherwise than as a trial court or the Court of Session;
- in England and Wales or Northern Ireland, the High Court or the Court of Appeal.

(s 4(5))

A declaration of incompatibility does not affect the validity, continuing operation or enforcement of the provision in respect of which it is given, and is not binding on the parties to the proceedings in which it is made (s 4(6)(a) and (b)).

Comment: Section 4 provides that where a compatible position has not been possible, the higher courts may make a declaration of incompatibility. Like s 3, this section draws a distinction between primary legislation and subordinate legislation which has its roots in primary legislation. If such a declaration is made, the effect of s 4(6) is not to invalidate the domestic law in relation to which the declaration has been made. The court is bound to continue to apply and enforce that domestic law. The declaration is, however, a signal to government to put right, if it chooses to do so, the offending legislation. The government may, however, decide not to do so. The Human Rights Act 1998 permits this.

The declaration is not binding on the parties. The government may disagree with the court's finding or may wish to appeal against the declaration. Section 4(6) – like s 3(2)(b) and (c) – is a significant provision which upholds one of the key themes in the Act – that of parliamentary legislative supremacy. Only the legislature may put right the offending domestic legislation; the courts must follow and enforce it until it has been changed.

Right of the Crown to Intervene

Where a court (as defined in s 4(5)) is considering making a declaration of incompatibility, the Crown is entitled to notice of that intention in accordance with rules of court (s 5(1)).

Under s 5(2), certain persons are entitled to be joined in the proceedings upon giving notice, again in accordance with rules of court. Those persons are:
- a Minister of the Crown or a person nominated by the Minister;
- a member of the Scottish Executive;
- a Northern Ireland Minister; or
- a Northern Ireland department.

Notice to be joined as a party may be given at any time in the proceedings (s 5(3)).

Any person who has been made a party to any criminal proceedings (other than in Scotland) by way of such a notice may, with leave, appeal to the House of Lords against any declaration of incompatibility made in those proceedings (s 5(4)). "Criminal proceedings" includes proceedings in the Courts-Martial Appeal Court. Leave can be granted either by the court making the declaration or by the House of Lords (s 5(5)).

Comment: The Crown retains the right to intervene in proceedings where a declaration is contemplated, because the complaint will be about domestic legislation for which the Crown is responsible. Clearly the Crown will have a view as to whether the legislation in question offends any of the Convention rights and will want to make representations.

There is a requirement in s 19 of the Act for a Minister responsible for proposed legislation to make a statement of compatibility of the proposed law with the Convention. Such statements will be based on the government's own research and any advice from experts. They should be based on genuine and honestly held views. Where an Act of Parliament, or indeed procedure, is challenged, it is not unreasonable, it is submitted, that the government be entitled to notice and to be a party to any proceedings in which compatibility is questioned. It may be that a court contemplating making a declaration will welcome the assistance afforded by intervention by the Crown.

Section 5(4) reserves to the government a right of appeal to the House of Lords if a court nevertheless goes on to make a declaration of incompatibility. Thus the Crown retains control of its own legislation.

There are examples, both past and present, of changes to UK law where it was out of line with Convention rights. Following the *Mal-*

one case in 1984, the government enacted the Interception of Communications Act 1985, and the Special Immigration Appeals Commission Act 1998 was passed subsequent to the adverse Strasbourg ruling in the case of *Chahal.*

The rulings of the ECHR in the cases of *T v UK and V v U, The Times,* 17 December 1999 (the *Bulger* case) led to the Lord Chief Justice's Practice Direction (Crown Court: Trial of Children and Young Persons), *The Times,* 17 February 2000. This Practice Direction lays down new procedures to be followed in trials of children and young persons in the Crown Court. The Practice Direction seeks to take into account the procedural aspects of the trial process which led the ECHR to rule that Article 6 had been violated.

Another aspect that concerned the ECHR in the *Bulger* case was the political or executive interference in the sentencing process which led the court to rule that Article 5 had been violated. As a direct result, the Home Secretary, Jack Straw, announced on 13 March 2000. that he would be referring the matter to the Lord Chief Justice, Lord Bingham, for him to set the "tariff". The trial judge had set a minimum sentence for Robert Thompson and Jon Venables – the two defendants – of eight years. The then Lord Chief Justice increased the tariff to ten years. The then Home Secretary, Michael Howard, increased it to fifteen years. This executive interference was said by he ECHR to offend against Article 5. See also *McKerry v Teesdale and Wear Valley Justices, The Times,* 29 February 2000.

In another recent ECHR case, *Caballero v UK, The Times,* 29 February 2000, the government had conceded that s 25 of the Criminal Justice and Public Order Act 1994 was not Convention-compliant. Section 25 effectively prevented courts from granting bail to a defendant charged with or convicted of murder, attempted murder, manslaughter, rape or attempted rape if the defendant had a previous conviction for such an offence. The petitioner was caught by this section in 1996. The original s 25 was amended by s 56, Crime and Disorder Act 1998, which came into force in September 1998, to make the section compliant with Article 5 of the European Convention of Human Rights, but the amendment came too late for the petitioner.

The process of legislative change to make domestic law Convention-compliant will continue where the government thinks it appropriate and necessary to do so. However, a change in domestic legislation or procedures may not always (and not automatically) take place. The government is not bound to act: it *may.* In areas of social policy or issues concerning public morality the government may want to retain existing domestic law and procedure. The risk is that these issues will then be resolved in the ECHR. The government would hope that on matters such as these the ECHR will allow a greater margin of appreciation (see Chapter 6).

It can be expected that this "honesty of purpose" in bringing domestic law and procedure into compliance with the Convention is to continue. Where appropriate, we can expect the government to change domestic law and procedures even without a declaration of incompatibility or an adverse Strasbourg judgment. There is, it is submitted, an expectation that those dealing with the Act and Convention will take seriously the need to ensure that the Act and the Convention rights do not fall into serious public disrepute. As Lord Steyn said in *R v Director of Public Prosecutions, Ex parte Kebilene and Others* [1999] 3 WLR 972:

"While passing of the Human Rights Act 1998 marked a great advance for our criminal justice system it is in my view vitally important that, so far as the courts are concerned, its application in our law should take place in an orderly manner which recognises the desirability of all challenges taking place in the criminal trial or on appeal . . . "

Although Lord Steyn was talking of a criminal case, it is submitted that the Act and the Convention should be applied in an orderly manner in all areas of the law.

Acts of Public Authorities

Section 6(1) provides that it is unlawful for a public authority to act in a way which is incompatible with Convention rights. This requirement does not, however, apply if the public authority:

- could not have acted any differently by reason of one or more provisions of primary legislation;
- was acting so as to give effect to or enforce one or more provisions of, or made under, primary legislation which cannot be read or given effect compatibly with the Convention rights.

(s 6(2))

A "public authority" includes:

- a court or tribunal, and
- any person certain of whose functions are public in nature.

It does not include either House of Parliament or a person who is exercising functions in connection with proceedings in Parliament (s 6(3)). The House of Lords acting in its judicial capacity is, however, a public authority (s 6(4)).

Section 6(5) provides that if an act of a public authority is private in nature it will not be caught by s 6(1).

"An act" can mean a failure to act, but does not include a failure to:

• introduce legislation or a proposal for legislation, or
• make any primary legislation or remedial order.

Comment: There is a more detailed treatment of "public authorities" later in this book (see page 145). Section 6 clearly places an obligation on public authorities to act compatibly with Convention rights. The s 6(1) duty is an interpretative one, which, when taken together with ss 2 and 3, makes the "interpretative obligation" complete.

The duty in s 6(1) does not apply where the authority is acting or is proposing to act in compliance with one or more provisions of primary legislation or provisions made under primary legislation. Although the public authority should act compatibly with Convention rights, if it cannot interpret domestic law so as to conform with the Convention rights, s 6(2) does not allow the authority to disregard its statutory duty under domestic law. The duty is still to uphold, apply and enforce domestic law. If there is any incompatibility, it is for Parliament, once again, to put matters right. Section 6(2) again reinforces the principle of Parliamentary legislative supremacy.

The Common Law
The combined effect of ss 2, 3 and 6 is to meet the requirements of Article 1 of the Convention through the "interpretative obligation", on the basis of which it is sought to make the Convention rights available in domestic courts. It is expected that there will be a high level of activity under the sections on interpretation. We also have seen that there is a constant and persistent theme running through these sections – the requirement that domestic law is not jettisoned or ignored. It is for Parliament to change the law if necessary.

We have also seen what the s 4(5) courts may do if they do find a piece of domestic legislation incompatible, and the effect of a declaration. We have also considered the role of the Crown, firstly, at the point where the Court is contemplating a declaration and, secondly, thereafter when a declaration is made.

The s 3 duty applies to the *interpretation* of legislation, and the power to make a declaration of incompatibility under s 4 of the Act relates to *legislation* itself. This leads to a consideration of the position of the common law. It is by no means clear how far courts are to be encouraged by the Act to develop the common law in new ways to give effect to Convention rights. Where the common law is incompatible with Convention rights, what is a domestic court to do? On the one hand, it is bound by the domestic principle of *stare decisi* and the formal system of precedence; on the other hand, it has the duty to act compatibly with Convention rights and to interpret legislation in a way which is not inconsistent with Convention rights. Yet the courts will be mindful that there is no provision in the Act to develop or to read and give effect to the common law so as to make it "Convention-compliant". It is submitted that what will emerge will be a strong duty on the courts not to act incompatibly with Convention rights. The Lord Chancellor said in Parliament that the judges were obliged to develop the common law consistently with the Act and the Convention rights (*Hansard,* HL, col 783, 24 November 1997):

> "We also believe that it is also right as a matter of principle for the courts to have the duty of acting compatibly with the Convention not only in cases involving other public authorities but also in developing the common law in deciding cases between the individuals . . . the courts already bring Convention consideration to bear and I have no doubt that they will continue to do so in developing the common law . . . s 3 requires the courts to interpret legislation compatibly with the Convention rights to the fullest extent possible in all cases coming before them."

We have already seen (page 6) how the courts, in developing common law, have relied on the presumption that the domestic law is not intended to violate the UK government's international obligations, and have applied international instruments in the domestic context. Courts dealing with the common law and its development will now have regard to the Human Rights Act 1998 and may feel a little more confident in this duty under s 6(1) as a public authority.

The court's obligation to act compatibly does not, however, extend to remedying the failure of the legislature to act, or to "filling gaps" left by the legislature. Legislation by means of developing the common law in the name of the s 6(1) duty is not envisaged. The courts are not required to act as legislators and are not required to provide new remedies for breaches of Convention rights beyond those under s 8, for example.

Although the Act formally restrains the courts and the judiciary, the requirements of s 6(1) strongly encourage the development of the common law in accordance with the Convention rights. Even so, the Act is silent as regards the common law. There is no power to make a declaration of incompatibility in respect of common law. On the other hand, there is no specific requirement in the Act to give effect to, to continue to apply, or to enforce the common law. Rather the contrary, because the court, as a public authority, is itself required to act compatibly and give effect to the Convention rights.

It is submitted that the interpretative obligation puts a real burden on the courts to find positions compatible with the Convention. It is not envisaged that there will be particularly frequent use of the declaration of incompatibility under s 4; such declarations are likely to be rare. Therefore, the burden of finding a compatible interpretation of legislation is a real one. The same may be so in relation to the common law.

Secondly, the duty in s 3 is to interpret legislation "so far as it is possible to do so . . . ". It is not a duty to interpret legislation so far as *reasonably* possible. It is submitted that the wording of s 3 requires a court to stretch itself to find a compatible interpretative position.

Thirdly, the general scheme of the Act is to make available in domestic courts the Convention rights, and the domestic courts in turn are to make them available to the citizen through the interpretative obligation. Any court faced with the prospect of concluding that a piece of domestic law is incompatible with the Convention (and therefore leading to the possible denial of Convention rights) will be under great pressure to find a compatible position. This approach will, it is submitted, be wholly consistent with the purposive thrust of the Act.

We can now move on to consider what happens when a public authority acts or proposes to act incompatibly with its s 6(1) duty. What follows is a review of the sections in the Act which give effect to the requirements of Article 13 of the Convention.

Proceedings

Section 7 provides that a person who claims that a public authority has acted (or proposes to act) in a way which is made unlawful by s 6(1) may:

- bring proceedings against the authority under the Act in the appropriate court or tribunal; or
- rely on the Convention in any legal proceedings,

but only if the person is (or would be) a victim of the unlawful act.

"Appropriate court or tribunal" means any such court or tribunal as may be determined in accordance with the rules (s 7(2)).

If proceedings are taken by way of judicial review the applicant will have a sufficient interest in the matter only if he or she is (or would be) a victim of the act in question (s 7(3)).

If proceedings are taken in Scotland by way of petition for judicial review the applicant will have title and interest to sue only if he or she is (or would be) a victim of that act (s 7(4)).

Section 7(5) imposes a time limit of "one year beginning with the date on which the act complained of took place; or such longer period as the court or tribunal considers equitable having regard to all the circumstances", but this is subject to any stricter time limit imposed in respect of the procedure in question.

"Legal proceedings" in s 7(1)(b) includes any proceedings brought by or instigated by a public authority, and an appeal against the decision of a court or tribunal (s 7(6)).

A "victim" for the purposes of s 7 is a victim only if he or she would be a victim for the purposes of Article 34 of the Convention if proceedings were brought in the Court of Human Rights (s 7(7)).

Section 7(8) provides that nothing in the Act creates a criminal offence.

"Rules" mean rules made by the Lord Chancellor or an appropriate Secretary of State or Minister (s 7(9)). Regard is to be had to s 9 when making the rules. The Minister or appropriate Secretary of State is empowered to make rules to add to the relief or remedies which a particular tribunal may grant, or add to the grounds on which it may grant such relief or remedies. This is likely to be done where the government takes the view that it is necessary to ensure that the tribunal can provide an appropriate remedy in relation to an act or proposed act of a public authority which is, or would be, unlawful under s 6(1). Any such order may contain incidental, supplemental, consequential or transitional provision. "The Minister" includes the Northern Ireland department concerned.

Comment: See pages 150–151 for further consideration of s 7. The "appropriate court or tribunal" was, at the time of writing, yet to be determined, and the rules yet to be made. This section creates new and directly enforceable Convention rights against public authorities and quasi-public bodies which have some public functions when they act in that public capacity. Firstly, it may create a new cause of action against public authorities which fail to act compatibly with the Convention. Secondly, it creates a new ground of illegality in proceedings brought by way of judicial review, i.e. failure to comply with a Convention right protected by the Act, although, obviously this is subject to the "statutory obligation" defence in s 6(2). Another view is that it does not create a new and fresh cause of action. It simply adds another limb to existing ones, ie, the remedy sought must already exist. Thirdly, a Convention right may be pleaded as a defence in a case brought by a public authority against a private body.

Section 7 does not, however, permit Convention rights to be used in a way which would override primary legislation. If domestic legislation is clear in its terms and clearly incompatible with the Convention the courts must nevertheless give effect to it. Equally, if primary (enabling) legislation prevents the removal of the incompatibility from the subordinate legislation made under it the court must give effect to and validate that law.

Judicial Remedies

Section 8(1) provides that, in relation to any act (or proposed act) of a public authority which the court finds is (or would be) unlawful, the court "may grant such relief or remedy, or make such order, within its powers as it considers just and appropriate".

Damages may be awarded only by a court which has power to award such damages or to order payment of compensation in civil proceedings (s 8(2)).

No award of damages is to be made unless, taking into account all the circumstances of the case, the court is satisfied that the award is necessary to afford just satisfaction (s 8(3)). The circumstances to be taken into account include any other relief or remedy granted by the court in question or any other court, and the consequences of any decision of that or any other court (s 8(3)).

In considering whether to award damages and, if so, in determining the level of damages, the court must take into account the principles applied by the Court of Human Rights under Article 41 of the Convention (s 8(4)).

A public authority against which damages are awarded is to be treated:

- in Scotland, for the purposes of s 3 of the Law Reform (Miscellaneous Provisions) (Scotland) Act 1940, as if the award were made in an action for damages in which the authority has been found liable in respect of loss or damage to the person to whom the award is made;
- for the purposes of the Civil Liability (Contribution) Act 1978, as liable in respect of damage suffered by the person to whom the award is made.

(s 8(5)).

"Court" includes a tribunal. "Damages" means damages for an unlawful act of a public authority. "Unlawful" means unlawful under s 6(1). (s 8(6))

Comment: See pages 151–152 for further treatment of s 8. This section is said to be the "remedies" section. Only those courts having power to award damages and compensation in civil proceedings will be allowed to grant such damages or compensation under this section. When determining the amount of any damages or compensation, the court must take into account the principles applied by the Court of Human Rights under Article 41. This is to ensure that an applicant is placed in the same or a similar position as if proceedings had been brought in Strasbourg.

Judicial Acts

Section 9(1) provides that proceedings under s 7(1)(a) in respect of judicial acts may be brought only:

- by exercising a right of appeal;
- by seeking judicial review;
- in such other forum as may be prescribed by rules.

This does not affect any rule of law which prevents a court from being the subject of judicial review (s 9(2)).

In relation to judicial acts done in good faith, no award for damages can be made unless an award of compensation is required to be made under Article 5.5 of the Convention (s 9(3)).

An award of damages under s 9(3) is made against the Crown, but no damages may be awarded unless the "appropriate person" is a party to the proceedings or has been joined (s 9(4)).

"Appropriate person" means the Minister responsible for the act concerned. A "judge" includes a member of tribunal, a JP and a clerk or other officer entitled to exercise the jurisdiction of the court. "Judicial act" means a judicial act of a court and includes an act done on the instructions, or on behalf, of a judge. (s 9(5))

Comment: Although this section allows an action to be brought in respect of judicial acts by way of an appeal or judicial review, or in such other forum as may be prescribed by rules, by virtue of s 9(2) this does not affect any rule which prevents a court from being the subject of judicial review. Section 29(3), for example, prevents the High Court from having jurisdiction over "matters relating to trial on indictment". Therefore, no judicial review lies in respect of a court's decision on a matter relating to a trial on indictment notwithstanding the provisions in s 9(1). There is some support for this proposition in *Kebilene and Others,* cited above. The House of Lords was dealing with an appeal from a decision of the Divisional Court, that the provisions under which the defendants had been charged ("reverse onus" clauses) violated Article 6 of the Convention. The House of Lords decided, *inter alia,* that judicial review did not lie in circumstances where a defendant wished to challenge a decision on the basis that his Convention rights were violated. The defendant's remedy lay, in the first instance, within the trial process and by way of the usual appeal process thereafter, and not through judicial review. The exclusion of judicial review of a decision affecting the conduct of a trial on indictment may avoid serious delay in criminal cases in which a defendant wishes to argue a Convention issue.

No damages may be awarded for judicial acts done in good faith otherwise than to compensate a person to the extent required by Article 5.5 of the Convention. An award of damages is made against the Crown, but only if joined in the proceedings.

Power to take Remedial Action
Section 10(1)(a) provides that s 10 applies when a piece of legislation has been declared incompatible under s 4 and, where an appeal, lies:

- those entitled to appeal have indicated that they will not do so;
- the appeal is time barred;
- the appeal has been determined or abandoned; or
- the Court of Human Rights has ruled against the UK and that ruling was made after the commencement of the Act.

Where a Minister of the Crown considers that there are compelling reasons to act under s 10 to remove an incompatibility, the Minister may make any order to amend the legislation in question to remove the incompatibility (s 10(2)).

If a Minister considers, in the case of subordinate legislation, that it is necessary to amend the relevant primary legislation, and that there are compelling reasons for doing so, the Minister may by order amend the primary legislation so as to remove the incompatibility (s 10(3)).

Section 10 also applies where subordinate legislation has been quashed or declared invalid by reason of incompatibility (s 10(4)).

Comment: This section comes into play after the court has declared a piece of legislation incompatible with the Convention, or where the Court of Human Rights has ruled against the UK. It is also clear from this section that a Minister need not wait for an adverse judgment from Strasbourg to activate the remedial "fast track" procedure if it is thought there is a need to remove or amend legislation to make it compatible with the Convention. This applies to both primary and subordinate legislation. This section should be considered in conjunction with s 20 of, and Sched 2 to, the Act on the "fast track" procedure.

Safeguard for Existing Human Rights

Section 11 provides that if a person relies on any provision of the Convention it does not prejudice any other right or freedom that person may have under domestic law; nor does it prejudice that person's right to bring any proceedings which could be brought outside ss 7 to 9.

Comment: This reflects the position that the Convention rights do not replace domestic rights and remedies; rather they co-exist and are in addition to those already available in domestic law.

Freedom of Expression

Section 12 applies when a court is considering whether to grant any relief which might affect the exercise of the Convention right to freedom of expression (s 12(1)).

If the person against whom the relief is contemplated is neither present nor represented, no such relief is to be granted unless the court is satisfied that the applicant has taken all practical steps to inform that respondent, or that there are compelling reasons why that respondent should not be notified (s 12(2)).

No such relief is to be granted the effect of which would be to restrain publication before trial unless the court is satisfied that the applicant is likely to succeed in establishing that publication should not be allowed (s 12(3)). The court is required to have particular regard to the importance of the right to freedom of expression; and, where the proceedings relate to material which the respondent claims, or which appears to the court, to be journalistic, literary or artistic material (or to conduct connected with such material), to:

- the extent to which:
  - the material has or is about to become available to the public, or
  - it is or would be in the public interest for the material to be published,
- any privacy code.

(s 12(4)).

"Court" includes tribunal and "relief" includes any remedy or order (other than in criminal proceedings) (s 12(5)).

Comment: This section preserves the right of freedom of expression in Article 10 of the Convention. Why the Act should single out this right (and the rights to freedom of thought, conscience and religion – see below) for extra protection in statutory form is interesting. The answer lies in politics. Inevitably, there were strong representations by and on behalf of the press during the passage of the Bill, resulting in this concession. Perhaps it is also an indication of the importance which the government attaches to this freedom.

As a result of this section it may be expected that *ex parte* injunctions to prevent publication will be rare. The section envisages that such applications will be made on notice unless s 12(2)(b) applies. This relief, before trial, will not be available where the court takes the view that in the final result the respondent will win the case. The courts are required to "have particular regard to the importance of the Convention right to freedom of expression". No such protection is given to the competing Convention right to "respect for private and family life" in Article 8. The section does not, however, override Article 8 and the right to privacy, which carries equal weight. It will be interesting to see how the courts will resolve the tension between these competing interests.

Freedom of Thought, Conscience and Religion

Under s 13(1), courts are required to have particular regard to the importance of the rights under Article 9 of the Convention (freedom of thought, conscience and religion) when determining any question arising under the 1998 Act if that decision will affect any religious organisation itself or its members collectively.

"Court" includes a tribunal (s 13(2)).

Comment: The reason the Act affords extra statutory protection to this right is, again, that there was strong lobbying during the passage of the Bill – this time by and on behalf of the churches and religious groups; this section is seen as a concession to them.

Derogations and Reservations

Derogations

A "designated derogation" under the Act means:
- the UK's derogation from Article 5.3 of the Convention; and
- any derogation by the UK from any article of the Convention or of any articles of the Protocols which are so designated for the purposes of the Act in an order made by the Secretary of State.

(s 14(1))

The current UK derogation is set out in Part 1 of Sched 3 to the Act (see pages 141–142).

If a designated derogation is amended or replaced it ceases to be a designated derogation (s 14(3)). The Secretary of State can, though, make a fresh derogation in respect of the article notwithstanding subs (3) (s 14(4)). The Secretary of State must by order amend Sched 3 to reflect any changes to the derogation (s 14(5)). A designation order may be made in anticipation of a proposed derogation (s 14(6)).

Comment: Article 15 of the Convention allows a member state, in time of war or other public emergency, to enter a derogation to deal with that emergency. A full explanation of the current designated derogation appears in Part 1 of Sched 3 to the Act.

The UK's designated derogation is in relation to the emergency situation in Northern Ireland. It remains to be seen whether the emergency will cease as a result of the peace negotiations at the time of writing.

Reservations

A "designated reservation" means:
- the UK's reservation to Article 2 of the First Protocol to the Convention, and
- any other reservation by the UK to an article of the Convention or of any article of any Protocol to the Convention so designated for the purposes of the Act and made in an order by the Secretary of State.

(s 15(1))

The current reservation is set out in Part II of Sched 3 to the Act (s 15(2)).

If the designated reservation is replaced or amended it ceases to be a designated reservation (s 15(3)). The Secretary of State can make a fresh reservation in respect of the article notwithstanding subs (3) (s 15(4)).

The Secretary of State must by order amend the 1998 Act to reflect any changes to the reservation.

Comment: The general scheme of many international or quasi-international treaties and documents is to allow member states to enter reservations to any part of the treaty or document with which that member state does not agree or to which it does not wish to give effect. A reservation is entered at the time that the relevant protocol is signed. A full explanation of the reservation entered by the UK appears in Part II of Sched 3 to the Act. There is a further explanation at page 142. The reservation entered by the UK relates to Article 2 of the First Protocol.

Period for which Derogations Have Effect

The general effect of s 16 is that the designated derogation, if not withdrawn, ceases to have effect at the end of the five year period beginning with the date of commencement of the Act. Any other derogation will cease to have effect at the end of the five year period beginning with the date on which it was made. Before the end of the five year period the Secretary of State may extend it by a further five year period. There are further technical rules in s 16(3), (4) and (5). If a designated derogation is withdrawn, the Secretary of State must make, by order, any amendments to the 1998 Act as the Minister considers necessary to reflect that withdrawal.

Review of Reservations

An appropriate Minister must review the designated reservation at the end of the five year period beginning on the date on which the 1998 Act comes into force. The Minister conducting the review must prepare a report on the result of the review and lay it before Parliament. There is a continuing duty to review the position every five years thereafter.

Appointments of Judges

The following may become judges of the European Court of Human Rights without being required to relinquish office in the UK:
- A Lord Justice of Appeal, Justice of the High Court or Circuit Judge in England and Wales;
- in Scotland, a judge of the Court of Session or sheriff;
- in Northern Ireland, a Lord Justice of Appeal, judge of the High Court or county court judge.

Such a judge is not, however, required to perform duties in the domestic courts while sitting as a judge in Strasbourg. There are other technical rules in s 18. Judicial pensions are dealt with in Sched 4 to the Act.

Statements of Compatibility

Under s 19, a Minister responsible for a Bill in either House of Parliament must make a statement of compatibility, before the second reading of the Bill, to the effect that in his or her view the provisions of the Bill are compatible with the Convention rights. If it is not possible to do so, the Minister must make a statement to the effect that, although such a statement cannot be made, the government nonetheless wishes the House to proceed with the Bill.

Comment: The Minister will have expert advice before making a statement of compatibility in relation to any proposed Bill. There are two considerations. Firstly, will a s 19 statement create a presumption that the Bill, and subsequently the Act, if passed, is Convention-compliant, or will the statement remain the Minister's opinion as to compatibility. It is submitted that the statement does not create such a presumption and that the statement will remain the Minister's "view", held honestly and based on expert advice. Some domestic legislation is so framed as to allow a presumption to be deduced, but s 19 is not such a section.

Secondly, a statement of compatibility under s 19 may be a helpful interpretative tool available to a domestic judge when considering whether a piece of domestic legislation is compatible with a Convention right, or when called upon to invoke s 3 of the Act. The judge may feel comfortable in the knowledge that the Act comes with the statement containing Parliament's intention that the legislation is Convention-compliant.

Subordinate Legislation

Section 20(1) provides that any orders under the Human Rights Act are to be made by statutory instrument. Remedial orders under s 10 of the Act will, likewise, be made by way of statutory instrument.

The provisions and procedures to be adopted are contained in s 20 and Sched 2 to the Act. Further consideration is given to this procedure at pages 147–149.

Interpretation, etc

Section 21 provides a helpful interpretation of some of the terms used in the Act. It is reproduced in the Appendix, page 168.

Short title, Commencement, Application and Extent

The Act is to be cited as the Human Rights Act 1998 (s 22(1)). Section 22 provides for some of the sections to have a commencement date much sooner than the rest of the Act. By virtue of s 22(4), s 7(1)(b) applies to proceedings brought by or at the instigation of a public authority whenever the act in question took place. Generally, that subsection does not apply to an act taking place before the Act comes into force.

The Schedules

Schedule 1
Part I sets out the Convention rights and freedoms. It is to be noted that Articles 1 and 13 do not appear in Part I of Sched 1. Article 1 is superfluous. As to why Article 13 was not included, see page 142.

Part II sets out the articles in the First Protocol that have been accepted.

Part III sets out those articles in the Sixth Protocol that have been accepted.

Schedule 2
In this schedule is set out the procedure to be followed when the "fast track" provisions are invoked.

Schedule 3
Part I explains, in detail, the current designated derogation entered by the UK.

Part II explains the designated reservation entered by the UK.

Schedule 4
This schedule deals with judicial pensions for holders of the office of an ECHR Judge.

Checklist
- The Convention rights do not have entrenched status under the Act.
- The Act "incorporates" the Convention rights only in so far as ss 2, 3 and 6 will allow.
- Not full incorporation of the Convention.
- The retention of parliamentary legislative supremacy.
- The Act does not make Strasbourg jurisprudence binding in domestic law.
- The Act recognises that the Convention rights are not entirely new to domestic law.
- The twin requirements of Articles 1 and 13.
- These requirements are met via ss 2, 3 and 6 and ss 7, 8, and 9 re-

spectively.
- The interpretative obligation under ss 2, 3 and 6.
- The non-inclusion of Article 13.
- Section 8, instead.
- Declaration of incompatibility (s 4).
- The effect of a declaration.
- Right of the Crown to be joined as a party to the proceedings in which a declaration is contemplated.
- The Crown's right to appeal against any declaration.
- A declaration could lead to the "fast track" procedure being invoked.
- "Fast track" procedure: s 10, s 20 and Sched 2.
- Actions against public authorities but only by a victim or potential victim.
- Compensation for breach of Article 5.5.
- No actions for judicial acts done in good faith.
- Statutory recognition of Article 10 rights – freedom of expression.
- Statutory recognition of Article 9 rights – freedom of thought, conscience and religion.
- The requirement to review the designated derogation and reservation.
- A statement of compatibility to accompany any new proposed legislation.
- The effect of s 22(4).

Chapter 5

The Convention Rights and Freedoms

The Classification of Convention Rights

Absolute and Qualified Rights

The substantive Convention rights can, broadly, be classified into absolute and qualified rights. To determine whether a particular right is absolute or qualified, Article 15 must be consulted in the first instance. It provides for derogation in time of emergency, and reads:

"1 In time of war or other public emergency threatening the life of the nation any High Contracting Party may take measures derogating from its obligations under this Convention to the extent strictly required by the exigencies of the situation, provided that such measures are not inconsistent with its other obligations under international law.

2 No derogation from Article 2, except in respect of deaths resulting from lawful acts of war, or from Articles 3, 4 (paragraph 1) and 7 shall be made under this provision.

3 Any High Contracting Party availing itself of this right of derogation shall keep the Secretary General of the Council of Europe fully informed of the measures which it has taken and the reasons therefor. It shall also inform the Secretary General of the Council of Europe when such measures have ceased to operate and the provisions of the Convention are again being fully executed."

An absolute right, therefore, is one from which no derogation is permitted under Article 15. Paragraph 2 of Article 15 sets out those articles which contain absolute rights.

It is also helpful to look at the wording and structure of each of the articles which contain substantive rights to ascertain whether an article establishes an absolute or a qualified right.

Article 3, for example, contains an absolute right to the prohibition against torture, inhuman and degrading treatment: "No one shall be subjected to torture or to inhuman or degrading treatment."

The wording of Article 3 should be compared with the wording of, for example, Article 8 which contains a qualified right to respect for private and family life. Article 8 reads:

"1 Everyone has the right to respect for his private and family life, his home and his correspondence.

2 There shall be no interference by a public authority with the exercise of this right except such as in accordance with the law and is necessary in a democratic society in the interests of national security, public safety or the economic well-being of the country, for the prevention of disorder or crime, for the protection of health or morals, or for the protection of the rights and freedoms of others."

Articles 9, 10 and 11 are similarly worded and structured. These are, like Article 8, typically qualified rights. Thus, the wording and structure of the articles containing qualified rights are important. The full text of the Convention is set out in Appendix 2 to this book.

Legitimate Aims

No restrictions or exceptions are permitted in respect of absolute rights. Articles setting out qualified rights contain, in the first paragraphs, the general rights (privacy, religion, expression, assembly), and, in the second paragraphs, the exceptions and restrictions. These exceptions and restrictions are what are known in Convention parlance and jurisprudence as the "legitimate aims". Thus, for example, where it is proposed to restrict or infringe a citizen's Article 8 rights to privacy the national authorities would need to establish one of the legitimate aims that appear in paragraph 2 of Article 8 – provided some other conditions are met, as to which see page 113.

A similar structure and catalogue of legitimate aims appear in the second paragraphs of Articles 9, 10 and 11, which set out what are being described here as typically qualified rights. The phrases, "in accordance with the law" in Article 8 and "as are prescribed by law" in Articles 9, 10 and 11, are, it is submitted, synonymous for all practical purposes. A common law lawyer, by virtue of training, instinct and upbringing, would be troubled by this difference in wording, spending much time "construing" each phrase and seeking an explanation for the differences. There is no apparent explanation. More importantly, perhaps, it has not caused any practical difficulty, as the Strasbourg jurisprudence has shown.

The Right to Liberty

Article 5 contains the right to liberty and security of the person:

"1 Everyone has the right to liberty and security of person. No one shall be deprived of his liberty save in the following cases and in accordance with a procedure prescribed by law".

There then follows a list (a to f) of instances under which the deprivation of liberty can be justified. This list is exhaustive. There are other rights in paragraphs 2, 3, 4 and 5.

Article 5 does not confer an absolute right. Derogation is permitted under Article 15. Indeed, we have seen that there is currently a designated derogation from Article 5.3 entered by the UK. Although embracing a qualified right, Article 5 is not like the typical articles containing qualified rights identified above; Article 5 does not include a catalogue of legitimate aims in any of its subsequent paragraphs. But there is an exhaustive list of instances, any one of which can justify deprivation of liberty.

The Right to a Fair Trial

Article 6 contains the right to a fair trial. There are a number of facets to Article 6 which, if adhered to, will lead to a fair trial. This article is difficult to classify and stands on its own given its nature and purpose.

It is submitted that the classification of the articles, although helpful, will not lead to a full appreciation of the way in which rights operate or how the European Court of Human Rights ("ECHR") approaches them. The contents, purpose and structure of each of the articles, and the jurisprudence arising out of each must also be appreciated.

Positive Obligation of the Member States

A key theme of the Convention is the principle of positive obligation. Member states have an obligation not only to observe Convention rights, but to have in place and to take positive measures, when necessary, to ensure that those rights are not violated by others. The Convention applies "vertically and not horizontally". This means that the Convention rights are enforceable as between individuals and the government and other emanations of state. This is so because the state is a party to the Convention and, as we have seen, Articles 1 and 13 puts the obligation on the member states. The twin obligations under

Articles 1 and 13, combined with the principle that the Convention rights must be practical and effective and not theoretical and illusory, give rise to this principle.

However, Convention rights are capable of violation not only by the state and its organs and public authorities, but by individuals as against other individuals. If the Convention rights are to be practical and not merely theoretical and illusory, a state cannot stand by and allow violations or potential violations.

Generally speaking, Strasbourg has left member states to decide for themselves how best to establish a legal framework and structures for the protection of those rights and the availability of remedies if those rights are violated. Where there are no remedies available Strasbourg will intervene.

In *Osman v UK* [1998] Application number 00023452/94, [1999] EHRLR 228, *The Times,* 5 November 1998, the family of the complainants had reported to the police that a teacher who had formed a disturbing attachment to, and infatuation with, their boy was harassing them and causing damage to their property. In the event the teacher attacked the boy and killed the father. The central complaint of the family was that the police had failed in their duty to bring an end to the behaviour of which they had complained.

Relying on previous binding authorities, the domestic Court of Appeal said that no action could lie in negligence against the police in the investigation and suppression of crime on the grounds that public policy required immunity from actions in court.

In the ECHR the family argued that their Article 2 and Article 6 (access to a court) rights were violated. The government argued that the claim should be dismissed because the family could not establish that in failing to take preventive measures there had been gross negligence or wilful disregard of the duty to protect life. The Strasbourg court analysed the positive obligation on member states pursuant to Article 2, and rejected this argument. It said, *inter alia*, that:

"such a rigid standard must be considered to be incompatible with the requirement of Article 1 of the Convention and the obligations of Contracting States under that Article to secure the practical and effective protection of the rights and freedoms laid down therein."

The court went on to say that it was:

"sufficient for an applicant to show that the authorities did not do all that could reasonably be expected of them to avoid a real and immediate risk to life of which they have or ought to have knowledge. This is a question which can only be answered in the light of all the circumstances of any particular case."

They went on to examine in detail the facts and circumstances of the case and concluded that there was no breach of Article 2 because the family could not point to any decisive stage in the sequence of events leading up to the shooting when it could be said that the police knew or ought have known that the lives of the family were at real risk.

The family had also claimed that their Article 6 rights (right of access to a court) had been infringed in that the domestic law was that, as a matter of policy, such claims should fail because the police had an immunity from prosecution as demanded by public policy considerations. This "exclusionary rule" applied to deny the family access to a court.

The ECHR went on to consider the applicability of Article 6. They concluded that Article 6 did apply in this case and that the exclusionary rule was a disproportionate restriction on the applicant's right of access to a court.

Although it is true to say that the ECHR is not prescriptive as to how member states should protect the Convention rights, or what remedies for violation should be available, some breaches of Convention rights are so fundamental that the ECHR will insist on certain remedies being made available. In *X and Y v Netherlands* [1986] 8 EHRR 235, the court insisted on having in place criminal sanctions for the type of Convention violation alleged. In that case a sex offence had been perpetrated by a male on a girl of sixteen years who suffered from a mental disorder. Under Dutch law no prosecution was possible because the girl was prevented from starting the criminal process.

The complaint to Strasbourg alleged that her Article 8 rights were violated. The Dutch government argued that since civil proceedings were possible they had not violated the girl's Article 8 rights. The court dismissed this argument and held that the civil proceedings were not enough for the sort of infringement that the girl had suffered. They went on to say:

". . . this is a case where fundamental values and essential aspects of private life are at stake. Effective deterrence is indispensable in this area and it can be achieved only by criminal law provisions; indeed, it is by such provisions the matter is normally regulated."

Another good example of the way in which Strasbourg applies the principle of positive obligation is the case of *Platform Arzte fur das Leben v Austria* [1988] 13 EHRR 204. Platform Arzte was an association of doctors who were campaigning against abortion in Austria and were attempting to bring about changes to the laws of that country. They had held several demonstrations which were disrupted by counter-demonstrators notwithstanding the presence of a large number of police. The association complained to Strasbourg that their Convention rights under Articles 9, 10 and 11 were violated because they were unable, effectively, to exercise their rights and freedoms of thought, conscience and religion, expression and peaceful assembly and association. Further, they claimed that the Austrian legal system did not provide an effective remedy under Article 13 to ensure effective exercise of those rights, and that the Austrian authorities had misunderstood the true meaning of freedom of assembly by having failed to take proper steps to ensure that the demonstrations passed off without incident.

The Commission had ruled the case to be inadmissible so far as Articles 9, 10 and 11 were concerned, but ruled it admissible so far as Article 13 was concerned.

The Austrian government claimed that because the Austrian state did not itself violate those rights it could not be responsible for any of the violations alleged by Platform Arzte; that Article 11 did not create any positive obligation on the state to protect demonstrations; and that the right to peaceful assembly was mainly designed to protect the individual from direct interference from the state when exercising that right. Further, Austria argued that Article 13 and the violation thereof depended upon the violation of a substantive article and a right arising under it. Because there was no violation of a substantive right, Article 13 did not come into play. The ECHR held:

(a) that the applicability of Article 13 was not dependent upon an infringement of a substantive right. It guarantees a remedy to all those who claim, on arguable grounds, to be victims of such violations;

(b) that in this case Austria did not fail to take reasonable and appropriate steps to prevent disruption of Platform Arzte's demonstrations and that no arguable claim could be made that their Convention right under Article 11 had been violated;

(c) that it is the duty of a member state to take reasonable and appropriate steps to allow peaceful demonstrations to proceed. However, they cannot guarantee this absolutely and they have a wide discretion as to what means are adopted. The court did not have to assess the expediency or effectiveness of the tactics adopted by the police in the circumstances of the case. There was no arguable claim that Austria had failed to take reasonable and appropriate steps.

That was the decision the Strasbourg court reached on the facts of the case. It went on to make the following observation in principle:

"A demonstration may annoy or give offence to persons opposed to the ideas or claims that it is seeking to promote. The participants must, however, be able to hold the demonstration without having to fear that they will be subjected to physical violence by their opponents; such a fear would be liable to deter associations or other groups supporting common ideas or interests from openly expressing their opinions on highly controversial issues affecting the community. In a democracy the right to counter-demonstrate cannot extend to inhibiting the exercise of the right to demonstrate.

Genuine, effective freedom of peaceful assembly cannot, therefore, be reduced to a mere duty on the part of the State not to interfere: a purely negative conception would not be compatible with the object and purpose of Article 11. Like Article 8, Article 11 sometimes requires positive measures to be taken, even in the sphere of relations between individuals, if need be."

The Rights

The effect of the Act is to make available in domestic courts the Convention rights. The Act guarantees, in Sched 1, the following rights:

Part I

Article 2:	the right to life;
Article 3:	freedom from torture or inhuman or degrading treatment;
Article 4:	freedom from slavery and forced labour;
Article 5:	the right to liberty and security of the person;
Article 6:	the right to a fair trial;
Article 7:	freedom from retrospective criminal laws;
Article 8:	respect for private and family life, and correspondence;
Article 9:	freedom of thought, conscience and religion;

Article 10:   freedom of expression;

Article 11:   freedom of peaceful assembly and freedom of asso-
             ciation, including the right to join a trade union;

Article 12:   the right to marry and found a family;

Article 14:   prohibition of discrimination.

Part II: The First Protocol

Article 1:   protection of property;

Article 2:   the right to education (subject to the reservation in s
             15);

Article 3:   the right to free elections.

Part III: The Sixth Protocol

Article 1:   abolition of the death penalty;

Article 2:   the death penalty in time of war.

Article 1

Although absent from Part I of Sched 1, Article 1 imposes a duty on
those states who have ratified the Convention to "secure to everyone
within their jurisdiction the rights and freedoms" protected by the
Convention. As we have seen, the inclusion of this article in Sched I
would have been superfluous, since those rights are available through
the scheme of the Act.

Article 2: The Right to Life

Article 2 provides that:

"1 Everyone's right to life shall be protected by law. No one shall be
deprived of his life intentionally save in the execution of a sentence of a court following his conviction of a crime for which this
penalty is provided by law.

2 Deprivation of life shall not be regarded as inflicted in contravention of this article when it results from the use of force which is no
more than absolutely necessary:

  a in defence of any person from unlawful violence;

  b in order to effect a lawful arrest or to prevent the escape of a
     person lawfully detained;

  c in action lawfully taken for the purpose of quelling a riot or in-
     surrection.

This is a most fundamental provision and is concerned with the protection of human life. The court will scrutinise deprivation of life with the greatest of care, particularly where deliberate lethal force has been used. This article prohibits intentional killing. The court will take into account all the circumstances, including the actions of the individuals who actually administered the force.

The Protection of Life
Article 2 imposes a positive duty to protect life as well as preventing states from taking life. With very limited exceptions this right cannot be the subject of a derogation under Article 15. The death penalty is not prohibited under this article provided that it has been lawfully authorised. Protocol 6 requires that the death penalty shall be abolished, but this Protocol is optional.

The Exceptions
The second paragraph of Article 2 sets out the exceptions to the right. The exceptions arise in the context of crime prevention and maintenance of law and order. The test is "no more force than is absolutely necessary". When such force is used in the defence of a person from unlawful violence, to effect a lawful arrest or to prevent the escape of a person lawfully detained, or in lawful action to quell a riot, deprivation of life shall not be regarded as being in contravention of this article.

In *Stewart v UK* [1984] 38 DR 162 a thirteen-year old boy was killed as a result of action taken by the army who had fired a plastic bullet into a crowd whilst controlling a riot. The Commission held that this was not a violation of Article 2. The force used was "absolutely necessary". It stated that force is "absolutely necessary" if it is "strictly proportionate to the achievement of the permitted purpose". Article 2 read as a whole indicates that the circumstances described in paragraph 2 do not allow for intentional killing, but define the situations where the use of force, resulting in an unintended deprivation of life, is permitted.

In *McCann v UK* [1995] 21 EHRR 97 several IRA members were shot and killed by the SAS in Gibraltar in 1988. The court held (by a majority of ten to nine) that there had been a violation of Article 2, ruling that the force used must be "no more than absolutely necessary" in setting out to achieve one of the exceptions in paragraph 2, and that the force used must be strictly proportionate. The idea of "planning and control" is important. The state is required to exercise strict control over its agents involved in operations where lethal force is likely to be used. It is also required to give appropriate training, instructions and briefings to its agents. One of the reasons the *McCann* judgment went against the government was that those controlling the operation allowed the events to take their course when they could, and should, have intervened. The soldiers themselves, it has to be recalled, were exonerated.

In *Andronicou v Cyprus* [1977] 25 EHHR 491 the police mistakenly believed that a gunman had more ammunition than he did. The gunman and hostage were killed by shots fired by the police. The court looked at the planning and control and ruled that the degree of force used was proportionate in pursuit of legitimate aims set out in paragraph 2 of Article 2. No violation was found.

In *Paton v UK* [1980] 19 DR 244, a husband attempted to prevent his wife from having an abortion. The Commission ruled the action inadmissible because "everyone" in Article 2 did not include a ten week old foetus, and that the life of that foetus was intimately connected with the life of the pregnant woman. The Commission was reluctant to say the life of a foetus of that age was separate from that of the woman. It had no viable life outside the mother.

In the case of *Osman v UK*, [1999] EHRLR 228, *The Times*, 5 November 1998, mentioned above, a teacher who had formed a disturbing attachment to a boy killed the boy's father. The police had been warned of the dangers by his family, who sued the police for damages for negligence. On public policy grounds the domestic court dismissed the case. No actions lie against the police for negligence in the investigation and suppression of crime.

The ECHR examined the state's positive duty to protect life. The court recognised that the police must be allowed to exercise their investigative powers in a manner which safeguards the principles of the rule of law and other guarantees which govern police action in investigating crime. These guarantees included guarantees under Articles 5 and 8.

The UK argued that before a violation of Article 2 can be established the family had to show that failing to take action against the teacher amounted to "gross dereliction or wilful disregard of their duty to protect life". Strasbourg rejected this argument and said, ". . . it is sufficient for an applicant to show that the authorities did not do all that could be reasonably expected of them to avoid a real and immediate risk to life of which they have or ought to have knowledge".

On the facts of this case the court found no violation. The police attached weight to the teacher's presumption of innocence. The police had taken the view that they did not have the degree of suspicion required to invoke their powers of arrest. The court said that the police were entitled to take that position on the facts.

However, the ECHR did not accept the domestic position which excludes the family, as a matter of public policy, from having access to domestic courts and denies them a remedy for breach of Article 2 rights. Such an exclusion was said to be rigid, and operated to deprive the family of effective protection to which they were entitled under Articles 1 and 2. The problem with the domestic rule, as far as the ECHR was concerned, was that it operated as an arbitrary rule and did not permit consideration of the merits of the case.

Article 3: The Prohibition of Torture, Inhuman and Degrading Treatment or Punishment

Article 3 provides that:

"No one shall be subjected to torture or to inhuman or degrading treatment or punishment."

No derogation from this article is permitted in any circumstances – even during war or public emergencies (Article 15). Article 3 imposes a negative duty not to inflict this sort of suffering, as well as a positive duty to see that the prohibited activities are not carried out within a member state's borders.

The ECHR has provided a useful starting point as to what can amount to torture, inhuman and degrading treatment or punishment. *Ireland v UK* [1978] 2 EHRR 25 was a case which involved the treatment of a prisoner involved in terrorism, in which the court defined the terms as follows:

a torture: deliberate inhuman treatment causing very serious and cruel suffering;

b inhuman treatment: treatment that causes intense physical and mental suffering;

c degrading treatment/punishment: treatment that arouses in the victim a feeling of fear, anguish and inferiority capable of humiliating and debasing the victim and possibly breaking his or her physical or moral resistance.

In each case the conduct must "attain a minimum level of severity" before this article is breached. Whether treatment has reached this threshold of severity will depend upon all the circumstances of the case. In particular, factors such as the age, gender and state of mental and physical health of the victim will be important. Commentators have suggested that mental anguish alone could amount to torture if it reaches a certain level of severity. The above should be regarded as a starting point and not be treated as an exhaustive list.

In *East African Asians v UK* [1973] 3 EHRR 76, the applicants were citizens of the UK and Colonies and they had been refused permission to join their wives in the UK. The Commission said:

". . . the racial discrimination to which the applicants have been publicly subjected by the application of . . . immigration legislation, constitutes an interference with their human dignity which . . . amounted to inhuman and degrading treatment . . .".

In *Cyprus v Turkey* [1976] 4 EHRR 482 it was said that actions of agents of states can breach Article 3. The allegation was that soldiers had raped women in Cyprus whilst on duty in that country. The court held the state responsible for the actions of the soldiers.

In *Ribitsch v Austria* [1995] 21 EHRR 573, the applicant claimed that he had received punches to the head, kidneys and right arm and kicks to the upper leg, at the hands of the police. This was held to be inhuman and degrading treatment.

In *Chahal v UK* [1996] 23 EHRR 413, it was held that a deportation order which could have serious consequences for the applicant at the hands of the receiving state could amount to a breach of Article 3. The Home Secretary said that a Sikh separatist, who was being held in custody pending deportation, was a threat to national security. The petitioner alleged that he faced the real risk of torture in India. The court found that deportation would violate Article 3.

In *Soering v UK* [1989] 11 EHRR 439, the court held that a deportation, the effect of which would be to put the applicant on death row for long periods of time, would violate Article 3.

In *A v UK, The Times,* 1 October 1998, a stepfather had chastised the applicant with a stick. The stepfather was charged with assault. He pleaded in his defence "reasonable punishment" and was acquitted. The ECHR held that there was a violation of Article 3 because the law failed to give adequate safeguards, insufficiently defining "reasonable punishment". As a result of the adverse judgment in this case, the government produced, in January 2000, a consultation paper on the punishment of children and the defence of reasonable chastisement – *Protecting Children: Supporting Parents.*

Tyrer v UK [1978] 2 EHRR 1, *Campbell and Cosans v UK* [1982] 4 EHRR 293 and *Costello-Roberts v UK* [1993] 19 EHRR 112 are Strasbourg cases which involved "corporal punishment". These cases emphasise the need to examine whether the punishment has reached the threshold which will lead to a breach of a Convention right. In *Costello-Roberts,* a rubber soled slipper was used to administer three strokes on the buttocks over a pair of shorts. The applicant had not adduced any evidence of any serious or long term effect. The court concluded that the minimum level of threshold required for Article 3 was not reached. This case was distinguished from others where the Article 3 threshold was reached.

It is to be expected that there will be a growing body of case law under Article 3. The areas of potential challenge involve cases on asylum, deportation, the rights of prisoners and conditions in prisons.

Convention rights apply to "everyone". This includes victims and vulnerable witnesses for the purposes of a trial. Courts and tribunals are public authorities, and so domestic procedures and law will have to be such as to ensure that the Convention rights of all that appear before them are protected.

Julia Mason, the petitioner in a case in the ECHR, contended that the domestic law did not adequately protect her Convention rights because it allowed a defendant conducting his own defence on a charge of rape to cross-examine her in person for five days. The Youth Justice and Criminal Evidence Act 1999 contains a series of measures designed to protect alleged victims in trials on charges of sex offences. At the time of writing it was expected that these provisions would be effective as of 1 April 2000.

Article 4: The Prohibition of Slavery and Forced Labour

Article 4 provides that:

"1 No one shall be held in slavery or servitude.

2 No one shall be required to perform forced or compulsory labour.

3 For the purpose of this Article the term 'forced or compulsory labour' shall not include:

    a any work required to be done in the ordinary course of detention imposed according to the provisions of Article 5 of this Convention or during conditional release from such detention;

    b any service of a military character or, in a case of conscientious objectors in countries where they are recognised, service exacted instead of compulsory military service;

c   any service exacted in case of an emergency or calamity threatening the life or well-being of the community;

d   any work or service which forms part of normal civic duties."

Article 15 permits no derogation from Article 4.1. Slavery or servitude is not the same as forced or compulsory labour. Slavery or servitude relates to a status ascribed to an individual and his or her station in life. Forced or compulsory labour relates to an individual who is required to do work under compulsion and under threat of punishment.

In *Van Der Mussele v Belgium* [1983] 6 EHRR 163, a young barrister protested that being made to do unpaid legal work violated his Article 4.2 rights. The crucial question which emerged was whether the pupil barrister had consented to carry out that work.

In *X and Y v Germany* [1976] 10 DR 224 it was held that an obligation to carry out legal work was not in violation of Article 4.2. Article 4.3 permits forced or compulsory labour in circumstances described in Article 4.3.a, b, c and d.

Article 5: The Right to Liberty and Security of Person

Article 5 provides that:

"1 Everyone has the right to liberty and security of person. No one shall be deprived of his liberty save in the following cases and in accordance with a procedure prescribed by law:

a   the lawful detention of a person after conviction by a competent court;

b   the lawful arrest or detention of a person for non-compliance with the lawful order of a court or in order to secure the fulfilment of any obligation prescribed by law;

c   the lawful arrest or detention of a person effected for the purpose of bringing him before the competent legal authority on reasonable suspicion of having committed an offence or when it is reasonably considered necessary to prevent his committing an offence or fleeing after having done so;

d   the detention of a minor by lawful order for the purpose of educational supervision or his lawful detention for the purpose of bringing him before the competent legal authority;

e   the lawful detention of persons for the prevention of the spreading of infectious diseases, of persons of unsound mind, alcoholics or drug addicts or vagrants;

f   the lawful arrest or detention of a person to prevent his effecting an unauthorised entry into the country or of a person against whom action is being taken with a view to deportation or extradition.

2   Everyone who is arrested shall be informed promptly, in a language which he understands, of the reasons for his arrest and of any charge against him.

3   Everyone arrested or detained in accordance with paragraph 1.c of this article shall be brought promptly before a judge or other officer authorised by law to exercise judicial power and shall be entitled to trial within a reasonable time or to release pending trial. Release may be conditioned by guarantees to appear for trial.

4   Everyone who is deprived of his liberty by arrest or detention shall be entitled to take proceedings by which the lawfulness of his detention shall be decided speedily by a court and his release ordered if his detention is not lawful.

5   Everyone who has been the victim of arrest or detention in contravention of the provisions of this article shall have an enforceable right to compensation."

The Nature of the Right

This article provides freedom from arbitrary detention and guarantees liberty. The right to liberty and security of person is to be read as a whole; in practice the two elements are rarely distinguished and should be treated as one right as opposed to two. Security of person does not relate to the physical and bodily integrity of the person, which is independent of the right to liberty. Articles 3 and 8 are more relevant in analysing issues concerning a person's physical and bodily integrity.

The right under Article 5 is not absolute and can be derogated from (under Article 15) in times of emergency. The purpose of Article 5 is to ensure that no one is deprived of liberty in an arbitrary fashion.

There are four important principles arising out of this article:

• No one can be deprived of his or her liberty except in accordance with a "procedure prescribed by law" (Article 5.1).

• The grounds upon which a person can be deprived of his or her liberty are set out in Article 5.1 a to f. This list is exhaustive.

- Any person aggrieved by a detention should be able to challenge that detention speedily (Article 5.4).
- Where a determination has been made as to a person's illegal detention in violation of this article, that person has an enforceable right to compensation (Article 5.5).

Deprivation of liberty can take place only under procedures "prescribed by law" (Article 5.1). This is designed to prevent arbitrary detention. It also means that the procedures set out by domestic law must have been fully complied with and the domestic law must be clearly formulated to allow a citizen to anticipate accurately the circumstances which could lead to detention.

When loss of liberty takes place further rights are activated. An arrest is lawful only if it is based on reasonable suspicion that an offence has been committed or that arrest is reasonably considered necessary to prevent the arrested person from engaging in offences, or fleeing after the commission of an offence (Article 5.1.c).

The purpose of the arrest must be to bring the person arrested before a competent court. The arrested person must be informed, in a language that he understands, of the reasons for the arrest and the charges (Article 5.2).

An arrested person shall be brought before the court "promptly" (Article 5.3). The arrested person is entitled to release pending trial. This can be on conditions.

Arrest and Detention

Article 5.1.a allows a competent court to detain a person after conviction. In order for a detention to be "lawful" there must be a court ruling, and lawful procedures must have been followed to effect the detention. A conviction means a determination of guilt. Article 5.1.a does not allow the ECHR, as a general rule, to review convictions and sentences imposed by the domestic courts. However, any such decisions will have to comply with Article 6.

Article 5.1.b allows for a person to be detained for failure to observe a court order, eg failure to pay a fine. The court order must be clear, the person must be given an opportunity to comply with the order, and the detention must be the only reasonable way of securing the terms of the order or obligation. Also permitted under this part of this article is lawful arrest and detention to secure the fulfilment of any obligation prescribed by law.

Under Article 5.1.c arrest is lawful if it is based on reasonable suspicion that a crime has been committed or when it is reasonably considered necessary to prevent crime or fleeing after a crime has been committed.

In *Fox v UK* [1990] 13 EHRR 157, an arrest had been made under the Northern Ireland (Emergency Provisions) Act 1978 which required a lower standard, viz, only a "genuine and honestly" held suspicion. This was found to be in breach of Article 5.1.c, the court holding that "genuinely and honestly" was a lower standard than "reasonable suspicion" which could lead an objective observer to hold that an offence may have been committed.

Murray v UK [1988] 11 EHRR was a terrorist case in which it was held that the purpose of the arrest must be to bring the arrested person before a competent legal authority. The fact that a person may not, in the event, be charged and brought before a court does not infringe this article because the purpose of the arrest is independent of the outcome of that arrest: *Brogan v UK* [1988] 11 EHRR 117.

Article 5.1.d deals with the detention of minors. The lawful detention of a minor is permitted if it is for the purposes of educational supervision. Detention has to be in accordance with a procedure prescribed by law. The detention of a minor is also permitted to bring him before the competent legal authority. This article allows a minor to be detained where it is necessary to secure his removal from harmful surroundings. Placing a minor in care would appear not to violate this article.

Article 5.1.e permits the detention of persons of unsound mind, people with infectious diseases, alcoholics, drug addicts and vagrants. These individuals can be detained because their release can sometimes endanger public safety, and their own interests and welfare may necessitate their detention: *Guzzardy v Italy* [1981] 3 EHRR 333. The fact that a person falls within one of these groups does not of itself justify detention. Detention has to be lawful and in accordance with a procedure prescribed by law.

Article 5.1.f concerns the prevention of unauthorised entry into a country, or deportation or extradition from a country. In *Zamir v UK* [1985] 40 DR 42, detention was held to be lawful because the purpose was to deport the applicant. Article 5.1.c conditions are not appropriate for a detention under Article 5.1.d. What is required is that the authorities are taking action with a view to deportation. Where the arrest and detention have been carried out in accordance with procedures prescribed by law that detention will be lawful, even if the sole purpose was deportation. If the deportation or extradition is unduly delayed or amounts to an abuse of power, the detention will cease to be lawful: *Chahal v UK* [1996] 23 EHRR 413.

The Right to be Informed

Under Article 5.2, every person arrested has the right to be informed of why he has been arrested and of any charge against him. This information should be in a language he understands. This article allows the arrested person to challenge the lawfulness of the detention. The information need not be in writing if the reasons are made clear during arrest. In *Ireland v UK* [1978] 2 EHRR 25, it was held that it was not enough to tell an arrested person that he was being held under the provisions of emergency legislation.

The Right to be Brought Before a Court

Article 5.3 requires that a person arrested shall be promptly brought before the court. In *Brogan v UK* [1998] 11 EHRR 117, detention for a period of four days and six hours was held to be a violation of Article 5.3. The aim of Article 5.3 is to impose a limit on the length of detention. What is intended is that "provisional detention of the accused person must not be prolonged beyond a reasonable time". Once the detention ceases to be reasonable the person must be provisionally released. What amounts to a reasonable period of detention is a matter of fact and degree.

The presumption is that bail should be granted unless withholding it is justified. The grounds for refusing bail are similar to those in Sched 1 to the Bail Act 1976. Any trial should take place within a reasonable time. (As noted in Chapter 3, Article 5.3 is subject to a UK derogation.) The Law Commission has published a consultation paper (number 157) entitled *Criminal law – Bail and the Human Rights Act 1998*.

The Right to Challenge Detention

Under Article 5.4, anyone in detention must be able to challenge the lawfulness of the detention. However, there are restrictions in relation to convicted persons.

A review must be by a court and must be prompt. In *Zamir v UK* (1985) DR 42 the Commission held that a period of seven weeks between an application for *habeas corpus* and a hearing violated Article 5.4.

Where detention is for long periods of time the detention must be reviewed at reasonable intervals: *Bezecheri v Italy* [1989] 12 EHRR 210. Article 5.4 requires a regular review of the lawfulness and the continuation of the detention where the circumstances of the detention change. *X v UK* [1981] 4 EHRR 188 was a case which involved detention on psychiatric grounds; the patient's six-month wait for a hearing before the Mental Health Review Tribunal was said to violate Article 5.4. In *Weeks v UK* [1987] 10 EHRR 293 it was held that a discretionary life sentence had to be reviewed. In *Thynne v UK* [1990] 13 EHRR 666 a review was required of the continued detention of young people convicted of murder. A similar finding was made in *Hussain v UK* [1996] 22 EHRR.

The principle which emerges from these cases is that where the reasons for the continued detention no longer exist, the legality of continued detention can be challenged. If re-assessment over a period of time shows that the extent to which the detained person is a "danger to the public" has diminished, that would seem to be a justification for a challenge.

The Right to Compensation
Article 5.5 provides that where a person has been detained in violation of Article 5.5, that person is guaranteed a right to compensation. This requires a binding award of compensation that can be enforced by the courts. The availability of compensation under this article is specifically preserved by s 9(3) of the Human Rights Act 1998.

Article 6: The Right to a Fair Trial
Article 6 provides that:
"1 In the determination of his civil rights and obligations or of any criminal charge against him, everyone is entitled to a fair and public hearing within a reasonable time by an independent and impartial tribunal established by law. Judgement shall be pronounced publicly but the press and public may be excluded from all or part of the trial in the interests of morals, public order or national security in a democratic society, where the interests of juveniles or the protection of the private life of the parties so require, or to the extent strictly necessary in the opinion of the court in special circumstances where publicity would prejudice the interests of justice.

2 Everyone charged with a criminal offence shall be presumed innocent until proved guilty according to law.

3 Everyone charged with a criminal offence has the following minimum rights:

    a to be informed promptly, in a language which he understands and in detail, of the nature and cause of the accusation against him;

    b to have adequate time and facilities for the preparation of his defence;

    c to defend himself in person or through legal assistance of his own choosing or, if he has not sufficient means to pay for legal assistance, to be given it free when the interests of justice so require;

    d to examine or have examined witnesses against him and to obtain the attendance and examination of witnesses on his behalf under the same conditions as witnesses against him;

    e to have the free assistance of an interpreter if he cannot understand or speak the language used in court."

The Nature of the Right

This article has featured in more applications/petitions to Strasbourg than any other article in the Convention. Article 6 is complex and has several different aspects. Although there are specific guarantees to those charged with criminal offences, parties in civil trials are not necessarily excluded from these rights. A glance at Article 6.1 will reveal that it is aimed at parties in both civil and criminal proceedings. Notwithstanding the applicability (on the face of it) of Article 6.2 and 3 to criminal proceedings, ECHR case law makes clear that the principles and standards of Article 6 also apply to civil cases. The principles of an adversarial hearing mean that rights in Article 6.1 will be the same whether proceedings are civil or criminal; see *Niderost-Huber v Switzerland* [1998] 25 EHRR 709; and *Lobo Machado v Portugal* [1997] 23 EHRR 79. The ECHR has stressed time and time again that its task is to determine whether a petitioner has had a fair trial, and in doing so it will look at the fairness of the proceedings as a whole, including the domestic appeal procedures if applicable. In looking at the overall fairness, the court will not, however, ignore fundamental and serious breaches of Article 6.

It has been said that the concepts "criminal charge" and "charged with a criminal offence" have an "autonomous meaning". The classification by a state of any proceedings is not conclusive. In *Benham v UK* [1996] 22 EHRR 293, a case involving the recovery of unpaid community charge, the petitioner alleged, *inter alia*, a breach of Article 6.3.c (legal assistance). Before he could do so he needed to establish that he was "charged with a criminal offence". In English law it is clear that he had not been charged with a criminal offence. The proceedings to recover unpaid community charge were civil in nature. However, the ECHR went on to consider the substance of the matter. The court held that the key questions were whether the proceedings were brought by a public body, whether they had punitive elements, and whether they had potentially severe consequences, and concluded that the proceedings were criminal in nature. Therefore, the protection under Article 6.3 should have been afforded.

The Minimum Requirements

There are a number of facets to Article 6.1 which go to make the minimum requirement:
- a fair and public hearing,
- within a reasonable time,
- by an independent and impartial tribunal,
- a public judgment, and
- a reasoned decision.

The press and public may be excluded where public order or national security may be compromised, to protect the interests of juveniles, or where publicity could prejudice the interests of justice. Judgments are to be pronounced publicly. The right to a public pronouncement is unqualified, and has been held to require that the judgment should be read in open court, as well as that the outcome should be publicly available.

Article 6.1 also requires that the hearing should be within a "reasonable time". What is reasonable will depend on the circumstances.

Further, Article 6.1 calls for an "independent and impartial tribunal established by law". This requirement implies actual impartiality as well as the appearance of impartiality. As these are minimum rights, further rights have been read into this article. These include:
- the right of access to a court,
- "equality of arms" (see below),
- the right not to incriminate oneself, and
- the right to effective participation in the proceedings.

In *Neumeister v Austria* [1968] 1 EHRR 91 the court introduced the concept of "equality of arms". This requires a fair balance between the opportunities afforded to the parties involved in litigation. Each party must be on the same level playing field. No party should be subjected to conditions that place the party at a substantial disadvantage in relation to the opponent.

Clearly this principle has implications for disclosure issues generally, and in particular in the context of criminal procedure. Adequate and timely disclosure will be a crucial pre-condition to a fair trial.

Crucial also to the concept of a fair trial are issues of evidence and admissibility. The court has taken the view that decisions about evidence are largely a matter for domestic laws and courts. In *Schenk v Switzerland* [1988] 13 EHRR 217, the court declared that the rules on admissibility are "primarily a matter for regulation under national law". And the task of the court is to determine whether the trial as a whole was fair.

The Presumption of Innocence

Article 6.2, which preserves the presumption of innocence, has been interpreted to include and support the privilege against self-incrimination. In *Saunders v UK* [1977] 23 EHRR 313, evidence from an investigative hearing at which the petitioner was compelled to answer questions had been relied upon in the subsequent criminal trial. The ECHR held that this violated his right to a fair hearing under Article 6.1:

> "The court recalls that, although not specifically mentioned in Article 6.1 . . . the right to silence and the right not to incriminate oneself are generally recognised international standards which lie at the heart of the notion of a fair procedure under Article 6 . . . "

In *Murray v UK* [1996] 22 EHRR 29, the court had to consider whether the adverse inference drawn when the defendant had exercised his right to silence was a violation of Article 6. Murray had been arrested under the Prevention of Terrorism (Temporary Provisions) Act 1989 and taken to the police station. In interview he said repeatedly that he "had nothing to say". He was not able to see his solicitor until after 48 hours. In later interviews he maintained his right to silence and said that his solicitor had advised him not to answer any police questions. The interviews were over a period of two days. Murray did not give evidence at trial and called no witnesses. The ECHR found that the drawing of inferences from silence did not infringe Article 6.2. But the failure to allow him legal access for two days at the police station did violate Article 6.3.c, even though the court concluded that the trial as a whole was not unfair.

Murray was a case where guilt had been decided by a judge sitting in the "Diplock Court" who had to give reasons. In the course of the judgment the judge had given detailed reasons for finding the defendant guilty, and had explained the inferences he had drawn. There was other strong independent evidence in the case. The position in respect of a judge's directions to a jury on whether they can draw inferences from silence is yet to be decided. At the time of writing, a decision by the ECHR on the merits of such a case is awaited in the case of *Condron* [1977] 1 WLR 827. Likewise, the position where guilt is decided by a jury, which may draw adverse inferences from a defendant's silence but is not required to give reasons, remains to be clarified. At the time of writing, a number of cases on the point are pending at Strasbourg. In *Murray,* the court found a breach of Article 6.1 in the denial of access to a solicitor during the first two days.

Although Article 6.2 appears to declare the presumption of innocence in an unqualified way, it is fairly clear that the ECHR is content to allow "reverse onus" provisions in certain circumstances. The extent and scope of those which are permissible have not yet been fully explored, and will depend to an extent on all the circumstances of the case and on how the prosecution intends to use such a reverse onus provision. Where domestic laws place an onus on the defendant to prove certain elements of his defence they do not necessarily violate Article 6.2: *Lingens v Austria* [1981] DR 171. Article 6.2 will not be breached where a presumption of law or fact is in favour of the prosecution and against the defendant. However, in *Salabiaku v France* [1988] 13 EHRR 379 it was held that those presumptions must be "within reasonable limits".

In *Salabiaku,* the defendant was convicted of importing drugs. In French law, once it was proved that the defendant was in possession of an article, there was a legal presumption that he knew what it was. The court held that this presumption did not violate Article 6.2 even though the offence was one of strict liability. Furthermore, the court held that the legal presumptions which effectively reverse the burden of proof on a particular point are not prohibited in principle, but that they must be kept "within reasonable limits . . . taking into account . . . what is at stake. . .".

In *R v DPP, ex parte Kebilene and Others* [1999] 3 WLR 972, an issue arose as to whether the provisions under which the defendants were charged violated Article 6.2 and the presumption of innocence. The relevant provisions were under the Prevention of Terrorism Act 1989 which "reverses" the burden. In the Divisional Court the Lord Chief Justice said that the provision(s) of the Prevention of Terrorism Act 1989 under which the defendants were charged undermined "in a blatant and obvious way" the presumption of innocence because of the reverse burden. The House of Lords was less sure. It rejected the claim on other procedural grounds and hinted that the issue may be resolved according to whether or not the reversal is of the "evidential" or "persuasive" burden. At the time of writing, the case has not been tried. It raises complex points of procedure and issues under the Convention and the Human Rights Act. Convention case law shows, however, that reverse onus clauses are permissible; see above, page 65.

Further Rights of Persons Charged
Article 6.3 contains further "minimum rights":

(a) The provision of prompt, intelligible notification of charges: the right of a person charged to be told of the case against him in a language that he understands. In *Fox, Campbell and Hartley v UK* [1990] 13 EHRR 157 the ECHR said that anyone who is arrested must be told:
> ". . . in simple, non-technical language that he can understand, the essential legal and factual grounds for his arrest, so as to be able, if he sees fit, to apply to a court to challenge its lawfulness".

(b) Adequate time and facilities to prepare a defence. In *Jespers v Belgium* [1981] 27 DR 61, the court described this as:
> "The right of the accused to have at his disposal, for the purpose of exonerating himself or to obtain a reduction in his sentence, all relevant elements that have been or could be collected by the competent authorities".

Whether, in a particular case, a defendant has had adequate time to prepare his case will depend upon the circumstances of the case. Where the lawyer appearing for the defence needs more time for the preparation of the case it may well be that an application to adjourn the case has to be made. This will be particularly so where there has been a late change in representation. What view the court takes regarding costs thrown away will depend on the circumstances. In *Goddi v Italy* [1984] 6 EHRR 165 it was accepted by the Commission that lawyers who step into the case late do so on the presumption that by virtue of their training they are able to cope. If they are unable to do so they would need to apply to adjourn the case or seek further time. This has clear implications for "returned briefs".

(c) *The right to representation and legal aid.* This comprises:
  • the right to defend oneself in person,
  • the right to legal assistance of the defendant's own choosing,
  • the right to free legal assistance if the interests of justice so require.
The general principles in this part of Article 6 include access to a lawyer and legal representation by a lawyer of one's choice, without charge where the defendant has insufficient means. The right extends to the pre-trial stage of a criminal case. This will ensure "equality of arms" between the parties.

Article 6 does not confer absolute and unlimited rights. There is no absolute or unlimited right to be consulted so far as legal representation is concerned. See *X v UK* [1982] 5 EHRR, *Croissant v Germany* [1993] 16 EHRR 135; *Ensslin and Others v Germany* [1978] 14 DR 64; *Goddi v Italy* (above).

In *Benham v UK* [1996] 22 EHRR 293, the court held that "where deprivation of liberty is at stake the interests of justice in principle call for legal representation". In *Murray*, cited above, the court held that Article 6.3 was breached where the defendant was denied access to a solicitor for 48 hours. Article 6.3.b and c underpin the principles of "equality of arms" (see *Neumeister,* above). Without adequate time and facilities and without legal representation, it is argued, there cannot be adequate equality of arms between parties to the proceedings. In the context of a criminal case, the principle of equality of arms means that the prosecution has to ensure that adequate and timely information is given to the defence at each stage of the proceedings in accordance with the case law on this principle.

(d) The right to the attendance of witnesses and to examine them or have them examined on the defendant's behalf. This is sometimes referred to as the right to confrontation.
This would, on the face of it, seem to deny anonymity to witnes-

ses. However, Convention jurisprudence seems to be that witness anonymity is permitted under certain circumstances, but the authorities emphasise the need for counsel to be able to observe the demeanour of each witness. The use of screens is not, generally speaking, in violation of this article either. This would be particularly important where it is necessary to preserve the anonymity of victims and vulnerable witnesses and their families because of the fear of reprisals. Where the defendant's right to challenge the witness's evidence is preserved and respected the use of screens and anonymity do not offend against the Convention. The Convention principles are set out in *Doorson v Netherlands* [1996] 22 EHRR 330 and *Van Mechelen v Netherlands* [1997] 25 EHRR 647. Domestic guidance can be found in *R v Schaub and Cooper, The Times*, 3 December 1993.

There is no express reference in the Convention to the rights of victims and vulnerable witnesses, but it is clear that the Convention rights apply to all persons within the jurisdiction and thus operate to protect victims and witnesses. In *Doorson*, the court held:

"It is true that Article 6 does not explicitly require the interests of witnesses in general, and those of victims who are called upon to testify in particular, to be taken into consideration. However, their life, liberty and security of person may be at stake, as many interests coming generally within the ambit of Article 8 of the Convention . . . contracting states should organise their criminal proceedings in such a way that those interests are not unjustifiably imperilled. Against this background, the principles of fair trial also require that in appropriate cases the interests of the defence are balanced against those of witnesses or victims called upon to testify."

It is clear from the wording of the Convention and the jurisprudence under it that the domestic courts, as public authorities, are required to be responsible for and balance the rights of defendants on the one hand, and those of victims and vulnerable witnesses on the other. It is only relatively recently that victims and witnesses have been recognised as having rights. Hitherto, those charged with managing the rights of victims and their families have been guided by public documents such as the *Victims Charter* and the *Child Witness Pack*. These documents have been helpful and have raised awareness of the way in which victims and vulnerable witnesses are treated in the course of a criminal case. It is submitted that the Convention rights applying to victims and witnesses should be seriously considered in weighing the balance. Both now have substantive and enforceable Convention rights to be protected by those who deal with them. It is further submitted that under the Convention there is a heightened duty to take into account and balance the competing rights.

Another issue under this article is the use of witness statements made by witnesses who are not present in court. Where the prosecution relied on statements without producing the witnesses to give evidence and be cross-examined, the court found a breach of the Convention, at least where the conviction was based "solely or mainly on the written statements": *Kostovski v Netherlands* [1989] 12 EHRR 434.

Sections 23 to 26 of the Criminal Justice Act 1988 permit courts to admit documentary hearsay in certain circumstances. This, it is said, is in contravention of Article 6.3.d. In *Trevedi v UK* [1997] EHRLR 520, the trial judge admitted, under these provisions, evidence in statement form from a patient who was medically unfit to give evidence in court. The challenge was on the basis that the defence did not have an opportunity to cross-examine this witness. The court held that the trial judge had made enquiry into the witness's condition and had directed the jury to give less weight to that evidence; that the defence had had an opportunity to comment on the statement; and that there was other evidence on which a conviction could be based.

It seems, therefore, that where the statements are "not the only evidence" against the defendant no violation would be found. Professor Ashworth in *Article 6 and the Fairness of Trials* [1999] CLR 261 suggests that it is important not to infer from the *Trevedi* case that ss 23 to 26 of the Criminal Justice Act 1988 are "Convention-proof". What the case demonstrates is:

". . . that in certain cases it will be possible to hold that the trial was fair, largely because of the strength of the other evidence. It does not alter the fact that the 1998 Act's provisions do not, on their face, comply with Article (3)(d)."

(e) Guarantees the right to an interpreter if the defendant does not speak the language of the tribunal.

Exclusion of Unfairly Obtained Evidence
There is no automatic right of exclusion of evidence to be deduced from Article 6. In *Schenk v Switzerland* [1988] 13 EHRR 217 the prosecution had relied upon evidence of a telephone conversation which,

as conceded by the Swiss Government, had been obtained unlawfully. The ECHR held that rules on the admissibility of evidence are "primarily a matter for regulation under national law". The court's task is to determine whether the trial as a whole was fair. The defendant had an opportunity to challenge the authenticity of the evidence in question, and it was "not the only evidence on which conviction was based". Thus, there was no violation of the right to a fair trial under Article 6.

In the case of *R v Khan (Sultan)* [1996] 2 Cr App Rep 440, the authorities had inserted a listening device into the wall of a house in which the defendant had been. The device recorded a conversation which implicated the defendant in serious drug activity. At his subsequent trial he sought to exclude the evidence obtained in breach of Article 8, weaving the Convention arguments into s 78, Police and Criminal Evidence Act 1984. The trial judge heard the arguments to exclude the evidence in a *voir dire* and applied the domestic rules on admissibility, ruling against the defendant. Mr Khan changed his plea to one of guilty.

On appeal, the House of Lords analysed the arguments, including the Convention arguments, and concluded that the evidence obtained in breach of Article 8 was properly admitted, citing the fact that the rules on admissibility of evidence were a matter for national courts. Lord Nolan said:

"I confess that I have reached this conclusion not only quite firmly as a matter of law, but also with relief. It would be a strange reflection on our law if a man who has admitted his participation in the illegal importation of a large quantity of heroin, should have his conviction set aside on the grounds that his privacy has been invaded."

He went on to say that it was astonishing that there was no statutory framework regulating the use of such surveillance devices by the authorities. At the time of writing, this case is awaiting judgment in the ECHR. The problem in the case, as Lord Nolan identified, is that it may not meet the requirements of the rule of law or legality discussed in Chapter 6 (page 129). Meantime, the government has introduced the Regulation of Investigatory Powers Bill to correct any outstanding issues of covert investigative work undertaken by the authorities and to make police investigations Convention-compliant. Intrusive surveillance is regulated by Part III of the Police Act 1997.

In *Teixeira de Castro v Portugal* [1998] CLR 751 a defendant who was not "pre-disposed" to, and who had no previous record of, drug dealing was approached by an under-cover officer who asked the defendant whether he could obtain some drugs. The defendant did so. He was charged and convicted. The court held that there had been a violation of Article 6.

Disclosure

Whether there has been any actual unfairness depends on the importance of the material disclosed to or withheld from the defence. Clearly, the duty on the prosecution is to disclose all material which undermines the prosecution's case and which assists the defence. This duty is a continuing one in domestic criminal proceedings. Disclosure is an important way in which the principle of "equality of arms" can be achieved as between the prosecution and the defence. The duty on the authorities is to investigate crime thoroughly and pursue all reasonable lines of inquiry, including those which point away from the suspect or the accused. The defence has a right of access to relevant material before trial.

In *Jespers v Belgium* [1981] 27 DR 61, the Commission said that the defendant should be allowed an opportunity to acquaint himself with the results of the investigations to enable him to prepare for his defence. The Commission went on to consider what is meant by "adequate" and concluded that the facilities are restricted to those that assist or may assist the defendant in the preparation of the defence. In *Jespers* the Commission said that the duty of disclosure extended to any material ". . . to which the prosecution or police could gain access". This clearly has to be qualified by the limitations on the powers of the police/prosecution to access, search and seize such material and the rights of others under the Convention. There is also a duty to disclose all material which may assist the accused in defending himself or in obtaining a reduced sentence. It is submitted that the Convention duty to disclose, in order that equality of arms be achieved, extends to remand hearings as well as to the trial process and beyond.

The court has, however, also held that, in general, the assessment of evidence is for the domestic courts: *Edwards v UK* [1992] 15 EHRR 417.

Three recent cases are relevant to disclosure and public interest immunity applications: *Rowe and Davis v UK, Application No. 28901/25, The Times*, 1 March 2000 (*R v Davis, Johnson and Rowe*

[1993] 1 WLR 613); *Jasper v UK,* Application No 27052/95, *The Times*, 1 March 20000; and *Fitt v UK,* Application No 29777/96, *The Times*, 1 March 2000. In the opinion of the Commission:

- in certain circumstances the withholding of material on grounds of public interest immunity is not offensive under the Convention;
- it is for the trial judge to ensure that the defendant receives a fair trial whenever material is withheld under public interest immunity. Whether a fair trial has taken place is a question to be determined in each case.
- the procedure of *ex parte* applications adopted in public interest immunity applications is an attempt to balance the interests of the state and the community against the interests of the defendant.

In *Rowe and Davis v UK*, a series of serious criminal offences, including murder, had been committed in December 1998 in Surrey. A substantial reward was offered for information leading to the conviction of the offenders. As a result of information received, the police were able to make a case against the defendants.

At the trial the prosecution relied on the evidence of a group of persons (the "Jobbins Group"). The members of the group gave evidence to the effect that some of them were responsible for stealing a car found abandoned at the scene of the first robbery and murder, and for having driven two other cars, stolen in the course of the last robbery, to a field in Sidcup where they had set fire to the cars. Members of the Jobbins Group gave other evidence which led to the conviction, in 1990, of the men charged.

The defence was that if there was anyone responsible for the crimes alleged it was the Jobbins Group who were unreliable as prosecution witnesses, and that their evidence was fabricated

On appeal to the Court of Appeal in 1992, the prosecution sought to withhold sensitive information on grounds of public interest immunity. These proceedings were *ex parte*. In 1993 the Court of Appeal reconsidered the issue of disclosure because defence counsel said it was wrong to have withdrawn from the hearing in 1992. Having heard defence submissions, the Court of Appeal ruled against the defendant and said the convictions were safe. In 1994 the defendants asked the Home Office to review their convictions. The case was transferred to the Criminal Cases Review Commission (CCRC) when it came into being in 1997.

In its report, the CCRC found, *inter alia*, that one of the witnesses who had given evidence for the prosecution was a police informant who had been paid a large sum of money and given immunity from prosecution in relation to his admitted participation as an accessory in the offences in question. This information was not disclosed to the defence or to the trial judge. (Much later, one of the other witnesses retracted his evidence.)

At Strasbourg, the Commission was of the opinion that the trial judge was in the best position to assess the public interest in non-disclosure when considering fairness to the defendants, and that the review by the Court of Appeal of the undisclosed material could not cure the absence of any examination by the trial judge. The Court agreed with the Commission in holding that there had been a breach of Article 6.1. It went on to explain that the trial judge who saw the witnesses give their evidence would have been fully aware of the evidence and the issues involved. The trial judge would have been in a position to monitor the need for disclosure throughout the proceedings as the evidence unfolded, assessing the importance of the undisclosed evidence. The trial judge would be aware of any new issues arising and the need to disclose if it would assist the defence to seriously undermine the credibility of prosecution witnesses which could lead to the defence case taking different directions or emphases.

The crucial question in this case was the absence of judicial control and supervision of the undisclosed material. As the court said, "In conclusion, therefore, the prosecution's failure to lay the evidence in question before the trial judge and to permit him to rule on the question of disclosure deprived the applicants of a fair trial . . .".

In *Jasper v UK*, the defendant was kept under observation by customs officers who followed him from his home. He collected an articulated lorry which he had bought some weeks prior to his arrest. He went to another location and loaded a consignment of meat onto the lorry, which he then drove into a lockup garage in East London. He drove away in his car, only to return several times to the lockup garage. On his final visit he remained in the lockup garage for approximately five hours. He was arrested as he was leaving.

Customs officers found that there were six pallets of meat still on the lorry in a frozen state. Four of the pallets, also containing a large quantity of cannabis resin, had been opened and left to defrost in the garage. The defendant told the customs officers that he worked for a haulage contractor, that he was unaware that the meat contained cannabis and that he was following instructions he had received by telephone the previous night.

The prosecution case was a strong one. The defendant had been caught red-handed with a large consignment of cannabis. He faced an indictment alleging an offence of being knowingly concerned in the fraudulent evasion of the prohibition on the importation of cannabis.

In January 1994, before the trial, the prosecution applied to the judge *ex parte* to withhold information on the grounds of public interest immunity. The defence were notified of the application, but did not know the category of the material the prosecution sought to withhold. The trial judge examined the material and ruled against disclosure.

The defence inquired of the prosecution, *inter alia*, whether there had been any material in their possession that had not been subjected to the *ex parte* proceedings, and in particular whether a telephone intercept or listening device had been used, and whether there existed any recording, note or memorandum. The prosecution took the view, rightly it is submitted, that it was not obliged to reveal to anyone whether there had been any interception of communication under the Interception of Communications Act 1995, and that any material falling under the Act should not be the subject of any *ex parte* application. Support for this proposition can be found in the Act itself and in *R v Preston* [1994] 2 AC 130. The trial judge had no power to order otherwise.

The defendant did not give evidence in his own defence and was convicted. At his appeal the Court of Appeal agreed with the findings of the trial judge and dismissed the appeal.

At Strasbourg, the Commission was of the view that there had not been a violation of Article 6.1 in that the petitioner did have a fair trial. It was convinced that the judicial control and supervision of the undisclosed material by the trial judge provided the defendant with the necessary safeguards. The judge was aware of both the contents of the withheld material and the nature of the defence case. The Commission did not consider that the non-disclosure of intercepted material rendered the proceedings unfair since it was not established that there had been any interception of communication or material arising therefrom. The principle of equality of arms was respected because neither the prosecution nor the defence could have used any intercepted evidence (the Interception of Communications Act 1985 prevents such use), and the petitioner could have given evidence as to the nature and contents of the telephone calls which he alleged took place, or called evidence from other sources as to the instructions he had received, but he had chosen not to give or call evidence.

The Court agreed with the opinion of the Commission and found no violation of Article 6.1. It further noted that the material that was not disclosed did not form part of the prosecution's case and was not put to the jury. The court was satisfied that the need for disclosure was at all times under the assessment of the trial judge who had the duty, throughout the trial, to monitor fairness to the defendant. He was fully versed in all the evidence and issues in the case and was in a position to monitor the relevance to the defence of the withheld material. The Court of Appeal had looked at the transcript of the *ex parte* application, which had revealed that the trial judge was "very careful to ensure and to explore whether the material was relevant, or likely to be relevant to the defence which had been indicated to him . . .". The trial judge had applied the principle clarified by the Court of Appeal that, in weighing the public interest in non-disclosure against the interest of the accused in disclosure, great weight should be attached to the interests of justice and the need for continued assessment of disclosure throughout the trial process.

In *Fitt v UK*, the prosecution's case was that the petitioner and several others were involved in a conspiracy to rob a Royal Mail van as it was due to leave a sorting office in Romford in East London. The group had relied on insider information. Unknown to them, the police were fully informed of the planned robbery. The police were observing the area and the defendants on the day of the robbery. Prior to the trial, the prosecution applied, *ex parte,* to withhold information from the defence. The defence was told that the information related to sources of information. The trial judge was told of the contents of the material in question. The trial judge had heard from the defence that if any such material would go towards establishing that there had been a "set-up", it should be disclosed. The trial judge did not order disclosure. He said that he had adopted the principle that if something actually would, or might, help further the defence he would order disclosure.

During the trial, the defendant C changed his plea to one of guilty. The jury was discharged and a new trial of the remaining defendants, including the petitioner, was ordered. In the meantime, C made a witness statement to the prosecution. The defence was informed and the Crown made a further *ex parte* application to the trial judge. Thereafter, the trial judge held an *inter partes* hearing as to whether the statement taken from C should be disclosed to the defence. To have disclosed C's unedited statement, which the trial judge had read, would be to reveal the sources of information. On that basis, it was agreed that the statement should be served in an edited form, omitting all references to sources of information. C was not called as a prosecution witness.

The petitioner was convicted. He later discovered that C had on many previous occasions given false information for reward. The petitioner appealed against conviction, and, in the Court of Appeal, sought an order that all previous statements made by C should be disclosed. The application was refused by the Court of Appeal, who said that it was not persuaded that there was any proper basis for ordering disclosure.

As to the undisclosed material at the trial and the statement of C, the Court of Appeal said that the trial judge was fully aware of the contents of the undisclosed material and of C's statement. The trial judge had indicated that he would order disclosure if it "did or might help the defence". The judge had carefully considered the matter before making a ruling. He had also considered the statement from C and had followed an alternative course proposed by the Crown, which was to provide a summary of the statement. The Court of Appeal saw no reason to interfere with the judge's rulings and dismissed the appeal.

At Strasbourg, the Commission was satisfied that the proceedings were fair because the trial judge was aware of the contents of the undisclosed material and the nature of the defence case. He was able to decide on the question of disclosure and to weigh the applicant's interest in disclosure against the public interest in non-disclosure. No violation of Article 6.1 was found.

The court agreed with the Commission and observed that the undisclosed material did not form part of the prosecution's case and was never put to the jury. The court was satisfied that the defence was kept informed and made representations in the decision-making process as far as was possible without revealing to the defence that which the prosecution sought to protect on public interest grounds. The important principle of judicial control and supervision of disclosure was observed. This issue was at all times under assessment by the trial judge, providing the petitioner with added protection because it was the judge's duty to monitor the fairness or otherwise of the evidence and material withheld. The trial judge was fully versed in all the evidence and the issues in the case and would have been the arbiter of fairness both before and during trial. In addition, said the court, the trial judge had indicated that he would order disclosure if it did or might help the defence, and the judge applied the principles clarified by the Court of Appeal that in weighing the public interest in non-disclosure against the interest of the accused in disclosure, great importance should be given to the interest of justice, and that it was important to continue the assessment of disclosure throughout the trial process. No violation of Article 6.1 was found.

These three cases illustrate perhaps rather well the ECHR's approach of dealing with each case on its own merits, and further illustrate that its judgments are facts-specific. There are, however, certain principles to be extracted.

In *Rowe and Davis* there was no judicial control or supervision of the need to assess whether to disclose the material which remained undisclosed. The material in question was never put to the trial judge and remained outside the judge's knowledge and therefore outside judicial control and supervision. The material was quite important, bearing in mind the nature of the defence. As the CCRC observed in its report, "if the jury had been aware of this then the credibility of the Jobbins Group might have been assessed in a more critical manner". Would it have made any difference to the jury's verdict if they had been told that one of the witnesses for the prosecution was an active informant who had been given immunity from prosecution?

On the other hand, in both *Jasper* and *Fitt,* there clearly was judicial control over and supervision of the question whether disclosure should be ordered. Furthermore, the undisclosed material was not to form part of the prosecution's case and was never put to the jury.

The principles that emerge from these three cases are:

- It is a fundamental aspect of a fair trial under Article 6.1 that criminal proceedings and procedures related to them should be adversarial and that there should be equality of arms between the prosecution and the defence.
- An adversarial trial means, in a criminal case, that both the prosecution and defence must be given the opportunity to have knowledge of and comment on the observations filed and the evidence adduced by the other party.
- Article 6.1 requires, as does English law, that the prosecuting authorities should disclose all material evidence in their possession for or against the accused.

- The entitlement to disclosure of relevant evidence is not, however, an absolute right. In any criminal proceedings there may be competing interests. These may include national security, the need to protect witnesses at risk of reprisals or the need to keep secret police methods of investigating crime. These considerations must be weighed against the rights of the defendants.
- In certain instances it may be necessary to withhold certain evidence from the defence so as to protect and preserve the rights of other individuals or to safeguard other important public interests, but the measures taken must be strictly necessary. To ensure that the defendant receives a fair trial any restrictions on the defendant's rights must be sufficiently counter-balanced by procedures which ensure that the defendant's rights are respected. The court referred specifically to the *Doorson* and *Van Machelen* judgments.
- Where material or evidence has been withheld from the defence on grounds of public interest, it is not the role of the ECHR to decide whether the non-disclosure was strictly necessary; as a general rule, it is for the national courts to assess such a matter.
- Where the evidence has never been revealed, as is often the case, the ECHR is not in a a position to weigh the public interest in non-disclosure against that of the accused in having sight of the material.
- The court's role is to scrutinise the decision-making process to ensure that, as far as possible, the adversarial nature of the proceedings is maintained, that there has been equality of arms between the parties and that the procedures adopted incorporate adequate safeguards to protect the interests of the defendant.
- There must be judicial control and supervision to assess whether there is a need to order disclosure before and during trial.
- The procedure which excludes the defendant and his representatives from the disclosure hearing – the *ex parte* proceedings – is acceptable and necessary in the public interest in certain circumstances.
- The ECHR confines its deliberations to the question whether the proceedings in their entirety were fair.
- "The jurisprudence of the English Court of Appeal shows that the assessment which the trial judge must make fulfils the conditions which, according to the court's case law, are essential for ensuring a fair trial in instances of non-disclosure of prosecution ma-

terial . . . The domestic trial court in the present case thus applied standards which were in conformity with the relevant principles of a fair trial embodied in Article 6.1".

• The Court of Appeal, in considering whether or not the material should be disclosed, provides an additional level of protection for defendants.

Article 7: No Punishment Without Law

Article 7 provides that:

"1 No one shall be held guilty of any criminal offence on account of any act or omission which did not constitute a criminal offence under national or international law at the time when it was committed. Nor shall a heavier penalty be imposed than the one that was applicable at the time the criminal offence was committed.

2 This article shall not prejudice the trial and punishment of any person for any act or omission which, at the time when it was committed, was criminal according to the general principles of law recognised by civilised nations."

This article is concerned with protecting individuals against retrospective criminal laws. It prohibits the punishment of acts which were not criminal when the acts were carried out. The article also prohibits the passing of a greater sentence than was in force at the time the crime took place. It requires legal certainty, seeking that criminal laws be framed with sufficient clarity to enable persons to distinguish between what is permissible and what is prohibited behaviour. The power to try and punish war criminals is specifically preserved, and the War Crimes Act 1991 is not offensive to Article 7.

This article applies to any "criminal offence". It has been noted above that under Article 6 the term "criminal offence" has been defined, in certain circumstances, to extend to cases classified as civil in domestic proceedings. Thus the term "criminal offence" is autonomous and independent of domestic classification.

In *Welch v UK* [1995] 20 EHRR 247 the defendant was arrested and charged in 1986 with drugs offences. By the time he came to be sentenced in 1987, the law on confiscating the proceeds of drug trafficking, the Drug Trafficking Offences Act 1986, had come into force. The defendant argued that this law would work retrospectively if he was sentenced in accordance with it. The UK maintained that the provision in question was not retrospective and not in violation of Article 7 because it was not a penalty under Article 7. Strasbourg disagreed and held that the retrospective application of the provision was a penalty and did offend Article 7.

In *Taylor v UK* [1998] EHRLR 90, however, a confiscation order that related back to proceeds amassed in 1974, in relation to drugs offences committed between 1990 and 1993, was held not to breach Article 7. The rationale was that by the time the defendant was committing drugs offences between 1990 and 1993 the 1986 Act was in force and the defendant was aware of the confiscation provisions. The Commission ruled the petition inadmissible.

In *Ibbotson v UK* [1999] EHRLR a convicted sex offender was required to register as such under the Sex Offenders Act 1997. This was held not to be a penalty under Article 7.

In *SW v UK* [1995] 21 EHRR 363 it was held that the common law was developing towards a position where it would be unlawful to engage in marital rape and, because the applicant could reasonably foresee this, his conviction for marital sex did not violate Article 7.

Article 8: The Right to Respect for Private and Family Life
Article 8 provides that :
"1 Everyone has the right to respect for his private and family life, his home and his correspondence.
2   There shall be no interference by a public authority with the exercise of this right except such as is in accordance with the law and is necessary in a democratic society in the interests of national security, public safety or the economic well-being of the country, for the prevention of disorder or crime, for the protection of health or morals, or for the protection of the rights and freedoms of others."

The Rights
The essential feature of Article 8 is that it protects the individual from arbitrary action by the public authorities. The right to respect for private life contains both positive and negative aspects, requiring not only that states refrain from interference, but also that they provide for effective respect for private life.

There cannot be an exhaustive list of what will fall into "private life". In recent years the concepts of "private life" and privacy have been given a broad interpretation. In *Halford v UK* [1997] 24 EHRR 523 the concept was extended to include privacy in the context of the workplace. The police had been bugging the petitioner's telephone at work. This was held to violate Article 8. This approach has allowed the court to extend the rights under Article 8 to personal issues such as sexual activity.

In *Dudgeon v UK* [1981] 4 EHRR 149 the court held that the criminalisation of all homosexual activities in Northern Ireland breached Article 8. In *Sutherland v UK* [1998] EHRLR 117 the Commission took the view that the different ages of consent between homosexuals and heterosexuals violated Articles 8 and 14. But in *Laskey v UK* [1997] 24 EHRR 39 the court found no violation of Article 8 where the applicants were imprisoned as a result of sadomasochistic activities. The activities were all consensual. The defendants in that case had been charged with offences including assault and wounding. A prosecution was not in violation of a Convention right because the state is entitled to take into account the potential harm that such activities can cause and this could be said to be in furtherance of the protection of health.

In *B v France* [1992] 16 EHRR 1, the court held that a transsexual had a right to have his or her changed sex recognised by the state. A refusal to allow a change to the birth certificate violated Article 8. But the court has taken a different view in *Rees v UK* [1986] 9 EHRR 56. This case was analysed in the context of Article 12 (the right to marry), which is much narrower in scope than the notion of family life in Article 8. The court in *Rees* (on preventing transsexuals from marrying) was unwilling to accept that the right to marry and found a family can exist outside the traditional marriage. Article 12 is concerned with procreation within the traditional family unit.

"Family life" is seen in its wider context. It is now considered to extend beyond formal relationships and legitimate arrangements. Any legislation which discriminates against children born outside wedlock is likely to be a violation of Article 8.

"The home" is protected under Article 8. Clearly, this will include one's right to occupy and enjoy its comforts without intrusion or interference.

"Correspondence" includes all forms of correspondence. Individuals have a right to uninterrupted and uncensored communications with each other. In *Malone v UK* [1984] 7 EHRR 14 the court found a violation of Article 8 when the UK intercepted the phone calls of the applicant. The court considered that since there was no statutory control of this activity it was therefore not in accordance with the law.

The case prompted the government to enact the Interception of Tele-communications Act 1985.

Communications and correspondence between prisoners and their legal representatives attracts Article 8 protection. Non-legal correspondence may be interfered with, but in *Silver v UK* [1983] 5 EHRR 347 the court stated that it will investigate these interferences to ensure sure that they are justified under Article 8.2.

Interference

As noted above, Article 8 is not an absolute right. An interference with an individual's Article 8 rights can be justified if it is "in accordance with the law" and if it is also "necessary in a democratic society". The interference must be to protect one of the "legitimate aims" in Article 8.2.

The requirement that any interference, either actual or potential, must be "in accordance with the law" allows citizens to determine in what circumstances their rights can be violated. In *Malone*, above, there was no legal basis, at the time, for telephone tapping. An interference should be "necessary in a democratic society". This means that there must be a pressing social need for that interference or violation, and that the interference or violation must be proportionate to the legitimate aim to be achieved.

The legitimate aims under Article 8.2 are:
- the interests of national security,
- considerations of public safety,
- the economic well-being of the country,
- the prevention of disorder or crime,
- the protection of health or morals,
- the protection of the rights and freedoms of others.

Article 9: Freedom of Thought, Conscience and Religion

Article 9 provides that:

"1 Everyone has the right to freedom of thought, conscience and religion; this right includes freedom to change his religion or belief and freedom, either alone or in community with others and in public or private, to manifest his religion or belief, in worship, teaching, practice and observance.

2 Freedom to manifest one's religion or beliefs shall be subject only to such limitations as are prescribed by law and are necessary in a

democratic society in the interests of public safety, for the protection of public order, health or morals, or for the protection of the rights and freedoms of others."

The Rights

This article provides for the right to hold religious beliefs and to change those beliefs, and the right to manifest them. The right to hold beliefs is absolute whereas the right to manifest them is not and can be restricted under Article 9.2. States therefore cannot limit freedom of thought. Strasbourg draws a distinction between the right to hold beliefs and the way in which they are manifested. Although a wide variety of religions and beliefs has been recognised, a narrow interpretation is adopted when this right comes into conflict with other considerations.

In *X v UK* [1981] 22 DR 27 the Commission held that the Inner London Education Authority, in not allowing a Muslim teacher to attend Jumma prayers on Friday, was not in violation of Article 9. This was so because he had not disclosed his wish to do so when interviewed for the job. The conflict was between the teacher's Article 9 rights as against the efficient operation of the school's timetable. The Commission said a fair balance had been reached.

In *Stedman v UK* [1997] EHRLR 545 the Commission decided that a requirement that a Christian work on a Sunday was not in violation of Article 9. The Commission dismissed the petition because the petitioner had been dismissed from her employment not because of her religious beliefs but because she refused to work the specified hours. In these cases the contractual rights of the employers seem to have taken precedence.

In certain cases, however, the ECHR has found violations of Article 9. In *Kokkinakis v Greece* [1993] 17 EHRR 397, Jehovah's Witnesses were prosecuted for propagating their beliefs and were fined. The court found that the activities engaged in by the Jehovah's Witnesses were a manifestation of their beliefs and thus attracted Article 9 protection. The court accepted that the prosecution was not proportionate because there was no pressing social need.

In a number of cases Strasbourg has rejected arguments that conscientious objections are not inconsistent with the Convention. Military service, for example, is compulsory in some countries. Thus, non-participation on Article 9 grounds will not assist the objector. In *McFeely v UK* [1980] 20 DR 44 Article 9 protection was not available to IRA prisoners claiming "special category status".

Limitations

Article 9 does not provide absolute rights. Limitations and restrictions can be justified under Article 9.2, but only in respect of manifestations of beliefs.

There is a requirement that any such interference or restriction of the rights and freedoms under Article 9 should be "as are prescribed by law" and "necessary in a democratic society". The structure of this article is similar to that of Article 8. It was noted above, in *Kokkinakis*, that the interference in question was prescribed by law. The legitimate aim invoked by Greece was the protection of the rights and freedoms of others, but the ECHR was not convinced that the steps taken were necessary in a democratic society in the sense that there was no pressing social need for the restriction.

The legitimate aims under Article 9.2 are:
• the interests of public safety,
• the protection of public order,
• health or morals,
• the protection of the rights and freedoms of others.

The legitimate aim "in the interest of national security" does not appear in Article 9.2; a state cannot restrict or interfere with a citizen's Article 9 rights on the basis of national security.

Article 10: Freedom of Expression

Article 10 provides that:

"1 Everyone has the right to freedom of expression. This right shall include freedom to hold opinions and to receive and impart information and ideas without interference by public authority and regardless of frontiers. This article shall not prevent States from requiring the licensing of broadcasting, television or cinema enterprises.

2 The exercise of these freedoms, since it carries with it duties and responsibilities, may be subject to such formalities, conditions, restrictions or penalties as are prescribed by law and are necessary in a democratic society, in the interests of national security, territorial integrity or public safety, for the prevention of disorder or crime, for the protection of health or morals, for the protection of the reputation or rights of others, for preventing the disclosure of

information received in confidence, or for maintaining the authority and impartiality of the judiciary."

Nature of the Right

This article has a special role and status ascribed to it under the Convention. It also has statutory protection (together with Article 9) under the Human Rights Act 1998, in recognition of the fact that one of the foundations of a democratic society is free speech and that the press and the media generally play an important role as the eyes and ears of the public. Any restriction or interference with this right will be closely scrutinised by the ECHR. In *Sunday Times v UK* [1979] 2 EHRR 245 the court said:

"The thalidomide disaster was a matter of undisputed public concern. . . Article 10 guaranteed not only the freedom of the press but also the right of the public to be properly informed."

In *Handyside v UK* [1976] 1 EHRR 737, freedom of expression is defined:

"Freedom of expression constitutes one of the essential foundations of a democratic society, one of the basic conditions for its progress and for the development of every man. Subject to Article 10(2), it is applicable not only to 'information' or 'ideas' that are favourably received or regarded as inoffensive or as a matter of indifference, but also to those that offend, shock or disturb the state or any sector of the population. Such are the demands of that pluralism, tolerance and broadmindedness without which there is no 'democratic society'. This means, amongst other things, that every 'formality', 'condition', 'restriction' or 'penalty' imposed in this sphere must be proportionate to the legitimate aim pursued."

Freedom of expression applies to a wide range of material, including political, philosophical, religious, cultural and other speeches and comments as well as artistic expressions. The medium through which they are expressed is not important.

Certain expressions will be better protected than others. Political speeches, for example, fall into a different category as compared with pornography. In a series of cases the ECHR has strongly disapproved, and has not afforded protection to, racist speech or literature. See as an example *Glimmerveen and Hagenbach v Netherlands* [1979] 18 DR 187. In *Handyside* the court went on to say:

"From another standpoint, whoever exercises his freedom of expression undertakes 'duties and responsibilities'. . . the court can-

not overlook such a person's 'duties' and 'responsibilities'. . ."
The right under Article 10.1 includes freedom to hold opinions and to receive and impart information and ideas. In *Gaskin v UK* [1989] 12 EHRR 36 the petitioner sought from a local authority certain records and documents held by the Social Services Department in relation to the period whilst he was in care. The records and documents fell into that category of material to which confidentiality attached. The domestic courts, following settled case law on the point, upheld the claim for confidentiality. The petitioner claimed in Strasbourg that his Article 10 rights were violated. In particular he said he had a right to receive information. The court, referring to an earlier case, held that:

> "the right to freedom to receive information basically prohibits a Government from restricting a person from receiving information that others wish or may be willing to impart to him. . . Also in the circumstances of the present case, Article 10 does not embody an obligation on the State concerned to impart the information in question to the individual."

Thus there had been no interference with Mr Gaskin's right to receive information protected by Article 10. Strasbourg went on to analyse the claim in terms of Article 8, and concluded that there had been a violation of the petitioner's rights under that article.

Although there is no obligation on governments or public authorities to disclose information under this article, no restrictions can be placed on individuals receiving information from those that are willing to impart it. There are clear implications for broadcasters. Restrictions imposed by way of licences and other requirements will not infringe Article 10 so long as the aim is to control the technical side of broadcasting, rather than the information which is broadcast. Action against those who operate without a licence will not offend against Article 10.

Restrictions

Article 10 is not an absolute right and follows the general structure of the qualified rights (in Articles 8, 9, 10 and 11). The rights discussed above can be limited or restricted under Article 10.2. Such limitations will be justified only if the requirements that they "are prescribed by law" and are "necessary in a democratic society" are met. Where measures taken to protect a legitimate aim are disproportionate, or where there is no pressing social need for them, it is likely that the court will find a violation of Article 10.

The legitimate aims that can be invoked under Article 10.2 are:
• the interests of national security,
• territorial integrity,
• public safety,
• the prevention of disorder or crime,
• the protection of health or morals,
• the protection of the reputation and rights of others,
• preventing disclosure of information received in confidence,
• maintaining the authority and impartiality of the judiciary.

Article 11: Freedom of Assembly and Association

Article 11 provides that:

"1 Everyone has the right to freedom of peaceful assembly and to freedom of association with others, including the right to form and to join trade unions for the protection of his interests.

2 No restrictions shall be placed on the exercise of these rights other than such as are prescribed by law and are necessary in a democratic society in the interests of national security or public safety, for the prevention of disorder or crime, for the protection of health or morals or for the protection of the rights and freedoms of others. This article shall not prevent the imposition of lawful restrictions on the exercise of these rights by the members of the armed forces, of the police or of the administration of the State."

The Rights

Three areas are protected by this right: freedom of peaceful assembly; freedom of association with others; and the right to form and join trade unions. Clearly, these are linked and overlap with each other.

"Assembly" covers demonstrations and marches both private and public. Where domestic laws requires prior notice of such an assembly to be given to the police, possibly with details of the route to be taken or allowing for the imposition of conditions, that will not offend against this article so long as the object is to ensure a peaceful assembly. Where it is clear to the authorities that a peaceful assembly is not possible, given the nature of the organisation involved or the opposition to it, or that the general climate is not conducive to a peaceful assembly, a blanket ban may be imposed. The authorities will need to be in a position to establish that fact by producing evidence.

In *Christians Against Fascism and Racism v UK* [1980] 21 DR 138, Christians Against Fascism and Racism (CARAF) was an association of people united in the love of God, whose function, *inter alia*, was to alert the public to the dangers of growing racism and fascist ideology. The organisation gave notice to the authorities of its intention to march in the city of London to draw the attention of the public to itself and to promote the aims of the newly formed organisation. This information was considered to be of particular importance at a time when the views of racist and fascist groups were receiving wide publicity.

The then Commissioner of Police in London, with the support of the then Home Secretary, banned "all public processions other than those of a religious, educational, festive or ceremonial character. . .". This ban was for a period of two months, and was considered necessary primarily because its immediate effect would be to prohibit a planned march in East London by the National Front. However, it had the effect of also banning the CARAF march, which was to have taken place after the march by the National Front.

The Commissioner explained that:

". . . by reason of particular circumstances existing in my police area the powers conferred on me . . . will not be sufficient to enable me to prevent serious public disorder being occasioned by the holding of public processions in the Metropolitan Police District."

CARAF petitioned the ECHR, invoking Article 11. The Commission found that in England at the time there was a tense atmosphere resulting from a series of riots and violence involving serious public disturbances occasioned by marches organised by the National Front and counter marches. Further marches had been planned. There was serious concern that public disorder would result. In these circumstances the Commission found the CARAF application inadmissible. The measures taken by the authorities were designed to ensure that no serious disorder resulted. The exercise of the Article 11 right to assembly could not be peaceful. The Commission had accepted that CARAF had no record of violence and that it was a peaceful organisation. Notwithstanding that, violence and serious public disorder by others gave the authorities real concerns that serious public disorder might arise.

Where there is no actual violence or the threat of it any sanctions imposed may violate Article 11; see *Steele and Others v UK* [1999]

EHRLR 109, and *Hashman and Harrop v UK* [1999] EHRLR 342 – see Chapter 6, page 132. Where individuals who are simply protesting about an issue are arrested on the basis that there is a likelihood of a breach of the peace, but there has been no actual or threatened violence, that may constitute a violation of Article 11.

Preventing individuals from forming or joining trade unions will be in breach of this article. The same applies to other forms of association.

Restrictions

The Convention permits states to place limitations on the exercise of these rights by members of the armed forces and the police as members of the administration of the state. In *Council of Civil Service Unions v UK* [1987] 50 DR 228 the Commission took the view that staff at GCHQ were "members of the administration of the state" and that therefore there was no breach of Article 11 in the decision of the UK to prohibit them from membership of trade unions. The restriction of the right was in respect of persons specifically mentioned in Article 11.2.

Article 11 does not provide absolute rights and shares the general scheme of the other articles conferring qualified rights, save that Article 11.2 mentions three specific groups of people. Any other restriction or limitation on Article 11 rights will need to be "prescribed by law", "necessary in a democratic society" and to protect one of the legitimate aims in Article 11.2. The legitimate aims are:
- national security,
- public safety,
- the prevention of disorder or crime,
- the protection of health or morals,
- the protection of the rights of others.

Article 12: The Right to Marry

Article 12 provides that:
> "Men and women of marriageable age have the right to marry and to found a family, according to the national laws governing the exercise of this right."

This article comes with no exception clause. "Family" in Article 12 is narrower in scope than under Article 8. Article 12 is focused on procreation within the traditional family unit. In *Rees v UK* [1987] 9

EHRR 56 the court was unwilling to recognise that the Article 12 right to found a family can exist outside of marriage, and maintained that preventing transsexuals from marrying does not violate this article. In *Johnston v Ireland* [1986] 9 EHRR 203 it was held that the right to marry did not carry with it the right to divorce.

Article 12 applies only to biologically opposite sexes, and the prohibition of marriage between homosexuals and transsexuals does not violate Article 12. In *Rees,* the court, denying a transsexual the right to marry, held:

> "the right to marry guaranteed by Article 12 refers to the traditional marriage between persons of opposite biological sex. This appears also from the wording of the article which makes it clear that Article 12 is mainly concerned to protect marriage as the basis of the family."

It is difficult to classify Article 12. Unlike Articles 8, 9, 10 and 11 there are no legitimate aims which can justify the restriction of this right. Domestic law governs not only the age at which persons become of "marriageable age", but also the rules applying to marriages.

Article 13: The Right to an Effective Remedy

Article 13 provides that:

> "Everyone whose rights and freedoms as set forth in this Convention are violated shall have an effective remedy before a national authority notwithstanding that the violation has been committed by persons acting in an official capacity."

The important aspect of Article 13 is that it is not included in Part I of Sched 1 to the Human Rights Act 1998. This is discussed in more detail at page 142. This article, read in conjunction with Article 1, establishes the twin requirements imposed by the Convention upon member states. An individual who has a claim that his or her Convention rights are violated should have recourse or access to an effective remedy. The merits and substance of such a claim should be examined and determined by a court. This will provide an aggrieved individual with an "effective" remedy. Where the allegation is one of breach, or a potential breach, of a fundamental right, the availability of an effective remedy may be of crucial importance. In *Chahal v UK* [1996] 23 EHRR 413, a deportation case, the issue was whether there was an effective remedy available to the petitioner under the judicial review process in respect of an allegation that, if deported, the applicant would face violations of his Article 3 rights (prohibition of torture etc).

Article 14: The Prohibition of Discrimination

Article 14 provides that:

> "The enjoyment of the rights and freedoms set forth in this Convention shall be secured without discrimination on any ground such as sex, race, colour, language, religion, political or other opinion, national or social origin, association with a national minority, property, birth or other status."

In practice this article is most likely to be invoked with one or more of the other substantive articles. In the case of *East African Asians v UK,* discussed at page 85, Article 14 was used in tandem with Article 3. The right not to be discriminated against applies to those who are treated differently but who are in similar positions. It follows that not all different treatment is discriminatory. In *Schmidt v Germany* [1994] 18 EHRR 513 it was established that racial or sexual discrimination will be justified only by very cogent reasons. Even if a particular form of discrimination can be justified, the principle of proportionality will apply.

Article 15: Derogation in Time of Emergency

Article 15 provides that:

"1 In time of war or other public emergency threatening the life of the nation any High Contracting Party may take measures derogating from its obligations under this Convention to the extent strictly required by the exigencies of the situation, provided that such measures are not inconsistent with its other obligations under international law.

2 No derogation from Article 2, except in respect of deaths resulting from lawful acts of war, or from Articles 3, 4 (paragraph 1) and 7 shall be made under this provision.

3 Any High Contracting Party availing itself of this right of derogation shall keep the Secretary General of the Council of Europe fully informed of the measures which it has taken and the reasons therefor. It shall also inform the Secretary General of the Council of Europe when such measures have ceased to operate and the provisions of the Conventions are again being fully executed."

This article allows for derogations from Convention obligations, but only "to the extent strictly required by the exigencies of the situation".

The UK has one derogation in place currently. It relates to the conflict in Northern Ireland and the Prevention of Terrorism (Temporary Provisions) Act 1989. The derogation allows the police to detain a person for up to seven days, and was entered following an earlier decision of the court that such detention was a breach of Article 5.3 of the Convention: *Brogan v UK* [1988] 11 EHRR 117.

In *Branningan v UK* [1993] 17 EHRR 539 the petitioner attempted to challenge the validity of the derogation entered by the UK. The court held that the UK derogation was validly entered and satisfies Article 15. Derogations and Article 15 are discussed at pages 141–142.

Article 16: Restrictions on the Political Activities of Aliens
Article 16 provides that:
> "Nothing in Articles 10, 11 and 14 shall be regarded as preventing the High Contracting Parties from imposing restrictions on the political activity of aliens."

This allows member states to restrict or interfere with the political rights of aliens. In *Piermont v France* [1995] 20 EHRR 301 the court said that members of the European Parliament cannot be aliens within any jurisdiction in the European Union. There, an MEP, who was also a member of the German Green Party, was invited by a local Member of Parliament to take part in an anti-nuclear and pro-independence demonstration in French Polynesia. The MEP was deported. She complained that her Article 10 rights were violated. Strasbourg agreed with her, maintaining that the right balance between preventing public disorder and her freedom of expression had not been reached.

Article 17: Prohibition of the Abuse of Rights
Article 17 provides that:
> "Nothing in this Convention may be interpreted as implying for any state, group or person any right to engage in any activity or perform any act aimed at the destruction of any of the rights and freedoms set forth herein or at their limitation to a greater extent than is provided for in the Convention."

Article 17 prohibits states from denying the rights and freedoms of people whom it considers to be extremists. At the same time it prohibits groups or individuals from seeking to invoke and rely on their own Convention rights and in doing so attempting to destroy the rights and freedoms of others. Article 17 has been successfully invoked in cases where racist or fascist organisations have incited racial hatred or circulated racist and fascist literature.

Article 18: Limitation on the Use of Restrictions

Article 18 provides that:

"The restrictions permitted under this Convention to the said rights and freedoms shall not be applied for any purpose other than those for which they have been prescribed."

This article is not unlike Article 14. They both operate in conjunction with one or more of the other articles, although Article 14 can have an independent existence. Article 18 can be violated with another article.

The First Protocol

Article 1: The Protection of Property

Article 1 of the First Protocol provides that:

"Every natural or legal person is entitled to the peaceful enjoyment of his possessions. No one shall be deprived of his possessions except in the public interest and subject to the conditions provided for by law and by the general principles of international law.

The preceding provision does not, however, in any way impair the right of a state to enforce such laws as it deems necessary to control the use of property in accordance with the general interest or to secure the payment of taxes or other contributions or penalties."

This article gives the right to peaceful enjoyment of one's possessions. It also allows the state to deprive individuals of their possessions and to control the use of possessions.

The concept of "possessions" for the purposes of this article has been interpreted widely and includes not only property and chattels but other interests such as shares, patents and goodwill.

The article draws a distinction between the deprivation of possessions and the control of such possessions. Deprivation of possessions is acceptable only if it is in the "public interest" and in conformity with international law and practices. The second paragraph of Article 1 of the First Protocol allows for the state to exercise a degree of control over possessions and their use. This is an acknowledgment that such interference is almost inevitable in a modern democracy. Legislation governing the relationship between landlord and tenant and rent controls are examples of state control over the use and enjoyment of possessions. Any fetter or interference on an individual taking up residence in his or her own property will be a deprivation of the right to use and enjoyment of one's own possessions.

Deprivation of the use or peaceful enjoyment of possessions without compensation will not be justified unless there exist exceptional circumstances. The article is, however, silent on whether compensation for such deprivation is to be awarded. Any deprivation must be for a legitimate purpose and a fair balance must be achieved between the competing interests: *James v UK* [1986] 8 EHRR 123.

Similarly, controlling measures over the peaceful enjoyment of possessions must have a legitimate aim and there must be proportionality between the measures taken and the aim to be achieved. Again, there must be a fair balance between the competing interests.

Article 2: The Right to Education

Article 2 of the First Protocol provides that:

> "No person shall be denied the right to education. In the exercise of any functions which it assumes in relation to education and to teaching, the State shall respect the right of parents to ensure such education and teaching in conformity with their own religious and philosophical convictions."

This article does not require the state to undertake to provide education. It exists to ensure that state intervention is limited or restricted in the arena of education. We find, therefore, the requirement that the religious and philosophical wishes of the parents be respected by the state and not interfered with. In *Belgium Linguistic Case (No 2)* [1968] 1 EHRR 252, the court held there to be a right, notwithstanding the negative tones in the first sentence of this article.

As noted on page 142, the second sentence of this article is subject to a UK designated reservation as it appears in s 15 of the Human Rights Act 1998. The reservation is explained in Sched 3, Part II to the Act:

". . . in view of certain provisions of the Education Acts in the United Kingdom, the principle affirmed in the second sentence of Article 2 is accepted by the United Kingdom only so far as it is compatible with the provision of efficient instruction and training, and the avoidance of unreasonable public expenditure."

Article 3: The Right to Free Elections

Article 3 of the First Protocol provides that:

"The High Contracting Parties undertake to hold free elections at reasonable intervals by secret ballot, under conditions which will ensure the free expression of the opinion of the people in the choice of the legislature."

This article applies only to the "legislature" and not to local government and the like. The right does not apply to referenda, and does not lay down rules for elections or prescribe any particular electoral system. See *X v UK* [1975] 3 DR 165 and *Lindsey v UK* [1979] 15 DR 247. *Mathieu-Mohin and Clerfayt v Belgium* [1998] 10 EHRR 1 sets out the principles. It emphasises the positive duty on member states to hold free elections, and that the rights protected are those which ensure that citizens have the right to vote as well as to stand for elections.

These rights are not absolute and can be subject to restrictions. Any such restrictions must not destroy the very substance of the rights.

The Sixth Protocol

Articles 1 and 2: The Death Penalty

Articles 1 and 2 of the Sixth Protocol provide that:

"1 The death penalty shall be abolished. No one shall be condemned to such penalty or executed.

2 A State may make provisions in its law for the death penalty in respect of acts committed in time of war or imminent threat of war; such penalty shall be applied only in the instances laid down in the law and in accordance with its provisions. The State shall communicate to the Secretary of the Council of Europe the relevant provisions of that law."

This Protocol requires the abolition of the death penalty other than in time of war or the imminent threat of war. The issue proved to be controversial during the passage of the Human Rights Bill, and the Sixth Protocol was added only after a free vote in the House of Commons.

The Government's White Paper, *Rights Brought Home: The Human Rights Bill*, October 1997 (Cm 3782) explained the Government's initial stance on the issue. In paragraph 4.13 it explained:

"The death penalty was abolished as a sentence for murder in 1965 following a free vote in the House of Commons. It remains as a penalty for treason, piracy with violence, and certain armed forces offences. No execution for these offences has taken place since 1946. . . The last recorded execution for piracy was in 1830. Thus there might appear little difficulty in our ratifying Protocol 6. This would, however, make it impossible for a United Kingdom Parliament to reintroduce the death penalty for murder, short of denouncing the European Convention. The view taken so far is that the issue is not one of basic constitutional principle but is a matter of judgment and conscience to be decided by Members of Parliament as they see fit. For these reasons we do not propose to ratify Protocol 6 at present."

As explained above, controversy over this position led to Protocol 6 being ratified. The pressure groups won the day.

Checklist

- Classification of the Convention articles.
- Absolute and qualified articles.
- Some articles – Articles 5 and 6 – are not so easy to classify.
- Classification of articles important, but note also the structure of the articles and the case law.
- Article 15.2.
- Importance of examining the wording of the article itself.
- An absolute article is one from which no derogation is permitted.
- Qualified rights are those from which derogations, restrictions and limitations are permitted, but only if certain condition are met.
- Importance of examining paragraphs 2 of the qualified articles.
- Positive obligation on member states.
- The Convention rights are contained in the Sched 1 to the Act.
- The permissible reasons/grounds for detention and loss of liberty

contained in Article 5.1.a to f are exhaustive.
- For breach of Article 5.5 the right to damages/compensation is specifically retained by s 9(3) of the Act.
- Many limbs make up Article 6.
- Article 6 does not create a rule of exclusion of evidence.
- The need to acknowledge and take into account the Convention rights of victims and witnesses.
- The need to balance the rights of victims/witnesses and those of, eg, the accused.
- The justification for any restrictions or limiting qualified rights can be found, usually, in the article itself, read in conjunction with the relevant case law.

Chapter 6

Limitations on Convention Rights

Introduction

The Convention rights are framed in wide terms. Some rights, as has been seen, are absolute and some are qualified. The text of the Convention needs to be examined to see if a particular right is absolute or whether it is subject to qualifications and limitations.

The Convention seeks to balance the rights of the individual as against other public and legitimate interests. An example is Article 8, privacy rights, as opposed to Article 10 on freedom of expression. The rights which engage the rights and freedoms of others are necessarily qualified, and the Convention permits them to be limited by the state. The Convention jurisprudence seeks to ensure that in the exercise of their rights the majority does not cause a disproportionate interference with the rights of minorities. There is always a need to balance the competing interests. Limitations and qualifications to the rights are permissible only if they are prescribed by law, intended to achieve a legitimate aim and necessary in a democratic society, that is, only if the measures taken are proportionate to the end to be achieved.

The European Court of Human Rights will inquire into whether an alleged breach of a right by restriction or limitation is prescribed by law; whether it serves a legitimate objective; and whether it is necessary in a democratic society. The scheme of the Convention is to allow interference or restriction of certain Convention rights, but only if a number of safeguards are met.

The Rule of Law/Legality

Article 5 allows for specified restrictions but only if they are "in accordance with a procedure prescribed by law". Article 8.2 allows for limiting or restricting the right contained in this article but only if it "is in accordance with the law". Articles 9.2, 10.2 and 11.2 allow for limiting or restricting the rights contained in these articles but only if such limitations or restrictions "are prescribed by law". These phrases, it is submitted, mean the same so far as Convention law is concerned. Together, they raise the principle of legality or the rule of law.

This means that state interference with a Convention right must derive its legitimacy from law; the state must act from a legal basis. The state must be able to identify, in the first instance, a domestic law authorising the interference. It must then show that the domestic law in question is accessible and that it is formulated with sufficient clarity. The purpose of this requirement is to ensure that those affected by such laws can learn about them and regulate their conduct accordingly. Thus, published law and rules will meet this requirement. Statute, common law and delegated legislation will meet the requirement of legality. It remains to be seen whether Home Office and other internal guidelines which allow for interference and restricting Convention rights will suffice to meet this requirement. In *Sunday Times v UK* [1979] 2 EHRR 245 the ECHR said:

> "The court observes that the word 'law' in the expression 'prescribed by law' covers not only statute but also unwritten law. Accordingly, the court does not attach importance here to the fact that contempt of court is a creature of the common law and not of legislation. It would clearly be contrary to the intention of the drafters of the Convention to hold that a restriction imposed by virtue of the common law is not 'prescribed by law' on the sole ground that it is not enunciated in legislation: this would deprive a common law State which is party to the Convention of the protection of Article 10.2 and strike at the very roots of that State's legal system."

The principle of the rule of law/legality is to ensure that interference in a Convention right is not arbitrary, and to act as a check on the use of arbitrary power. Hence the requirement for the law to be accessible. However, the fact that a citizen has to consult a lawyer will not lead the court to find a breach of this rule. In the *Sunday Times* case the court said:

> "In the court's opinion, the following are two of the requirements that flow from the expression 'prescribed by law'. First, the law must be adequately accessible: the citizen must be able to have an

indication that is adequate in the circumstances of the legal rules applicable to a given case. Secondly, a norm cannot be regarded as a 'law' unless it is formulated with sufficient precision to enable the citizen to regulate his conduct: he must be able – if need be with appropriate advice – to foresee, to a degree that is reasonable in the circumstances, the consequences which a given action may entail. Those consequences need not be foreseen with absolute certainty: experience shows this to be unattainable. Again, whilst certainty is highly desirable, it may bring in its train excessive rigidity and the law must be able to keep pace with changing circumstances. Accordingly, many laws are inevitably couched in terms which, to a greater or lesser extent, are vague and whose interpretation and application are questions of practice."

In the *Sunday Times* case the issue was, *inter alia*, whether the then law on contempt of court in the domestic context met the requirements of the principle of legality or the rule of law. The court went on to find that the law of contempt of court in the UK, at the time, was formulated with sufficient precision to allow the applicants to foresee to a reasonable degree that their article might constitute a breach of the law of contempt of court. Other Convention principles were discussed in the case, as to which see below.

The fact that the common law may be evolving and may change will not lead to breach of the rule. This is in recognition of the dynamic nature of the law to take account of changing needs. In *SW and CR v UK* [1996] 21 EHRR 363, the ECHR held that where the development of the common law was reasonably foreseeable the rule of certainty was not breached. In that case the court said that the common law was evolving to a position whereby husbands who raped their wives would be subject to the full rigours of a criminal prosecution. Because that was reasonably foreseeable, no breach of Article 7 (no retrospective criminal laws or punishment) was found. Absolute certainty of the law is not required. Reasonable certainty will suffice.

There is no requirement that state authorities inform individuals as to when authorities are likely to act. There is no requirement that individuals be notified when a particular set of rules is aimed at them.

An example of a case in which the principle of legality was not met is *Malone v UK* [1984] 7 EHRR 14. The petitioner's telephone calls were intercepted during an investigation. At the time there was no law regulating such activity. The practice of telephone intercepts was governed only by Home Office guidelines and other internal procedures. The ECHR found that this failed to meet the Convention test of the rule of law or legality. As noted above, the Interception of Communications Act 1985 was enacted as a result of the judgment.

In *Hashman and Harrup v UK* [1999] EHRLR 342 two hunt saboteurs were bound over to be of good behaviour for a period of twelve months. The two applicants had disturbed the Portman Hunt in March 1993. They appealed to the Crown Court. In April 1994 one applicant was found to have blown the hunting horn and the other to have shouted at the hounds. The Crown Court held that the actions were a deliberate attempt to disrupt the hunt, unlawful and put the hounds in danger. It considered that as there was no violence or the threat of it there had been no breach of the peace. The behaviour was said to be *contra bono mores* – "wrong rather than right in the judgment of the majority of contemporary fellow citizens". As a result they were bound over.

The petitioners complained to the ECHR, *inter alia*, that their Article 10 rights (freedom of expression) had been violated, and that the idea of behaviour *contra bono mores* was so vague and broad that it did not comply with the requirement of Article 10.2 that any interference with the right must be "prescribed by law". The court agreed that on the facts of the case there had been a violation of Article 10. The court appears to have been influenced by the fact that "behaviour which was wrong rather than right in the judgment of the majority of contemporary citizens" was not defined, and by the fact that no breach of the peace had been found.

Relying on the principles in the *Sunday Times* case, the court went on to find that "the binding-over order in the present case thus had purely prospective effect. It did not require a finding that there had been a breach of the peace". The court differentiated the case of *Steel and Others v UK* [1998] *The Times,* 1 October 1998, in which there had been a finding of a breach of the peace against the applicants. The distinction is that in *Hashman and Harrop* the applicants did not breach the peace, whereas in *Steel* the applicants had been found to have done so. Therefore, Hashman and Harrop could not be clear as to what behaviour they should avoid in future. In both judgments the ECHR accepted the power of the domestic courts to impose a bindover, either on a person admitting a breach or upon a finding by the court. The court also acknowledged the power of the domestic court to impose a bindover as part of a sentence after conviction of a criminal offence following a trial. It follows that *Hashman and Harrop* does not lay down, and is not an authority for, the proposition that a bindover to be of good behaviour in the future is contrary to Convention principles.

It is submitted that *Hashman and Harrup*, like all Strasbourg judgments, should be seen in the particular factual contexts in which the cases arose. Not all cases in which a bindover has been imposed will lead to an automatic finding that the requirements of "prescribed by law" have not been satisfied.

Legitimate Aims

Any interference by a public authority or a state with a Convention right must be directed towards an identifiable legitimate aim. The second parts of Articles 8, 9, 10 and 11 set out the legitimate aims. Interests of public safety, national security, protection of health and morals, the economic well-being of a country, or the protection of the rights and freedoms of others are all examples of legitimate aims which can be pleaded as a defence by a public authority or a state. Identified in the last chapter were the relevant legitimate aims as they relate to each of the articles. It is, therefore, not difficult for a State to find reasons and justifications for interfering with a Convention right. More than one legitimate aim can be claimed by a state, although only one is necessary to defeat a claim.

Proportionality

An important principle used by the ECHR in assessing if a right has been improperly violated is that of proportionality. Paragraphs 2 of Articles 8, 9, 10 and 11 each, as has been seen, allow for restrictions of or interference with Convention rights if done "in accordance with the law" or if "prescribed by law". The same paragraphs include the words "and are necessary in a democratic society".

Once the state can establish the rule of law and legitimacy, it has to point to one of the legitimate aims that it seeks to protect. Having done that, it needs to establish that the measures it has adopted to restrict or interfere with a Convention right are proportionate. The Convention requires an interference with a right to be "proportionate to the legitimate aim pursued": *Handyside v UK* [1976] 1 EHRR 737.

This means that an interference in pursuit of a legitimate aim in itself will not be justified if the means adopted are extreme or excessive in the circumstances. The concept of proportionality is designed to prevent states using a sledge-hammer to crack a nut – a familiar concept in domestic law. In *Soering v UK* [1989] 11 EHRR 439 the court explained the concept in this way:

> ". . . inherent in the whole of the Convention is a search for a fair balance between the demands of the general interest of the community and the requirements of the protection of the individual's human rights."

The principle of proportionality is a key feature of the Strasbourg case law. A fair balance between the overall needs of the community and the citizen's human rights can be achieved only if the measures adopted are strictly proportionate to the legitimate aim invoked. The principle of proportionality has been developed in the Strasbourg jurisprudence. It does not feature in the language of the Convention. Proportionality is about minimum intervention in Convention rights relative to the harm that may result from not interfering. The ECHR, in analysing the cases which come before it, will ask whether what was done was the only and best way to deal with the matter, having regard to the rights of others.

Dudgeon v UK

Thus, any interference must be justified by a legitimate aim and proportionate to the need at hand; and necessary in a democratic society (a democratic society is one which is pluralistic, tolerant and broad minded). In *Dudgeon v UK* [1981] 4 EHRR 149 the ECHR explained that "necessary" in the context of the Convention does not mean, and does not have the flexibility of expressions such as, "useful" or "reasonable" or "desirable". The court interprets the phrase to mean that there must be "a pressing social need" for the interference. Although the phrases are not defined in the Convention their meanings are discernible from the case law.

The case law also demonstrates how the concepts of the rule of law or legitimacy, legitimate aims, proportionality (necessary in a democratic society) and pressing social need are applied to any given complaint.

In *Dudgeon v UK* the petitioner challenged the then law in Northern Ireland which made buggery between consenting gay males a criminal offence. The court held that the law violated Article 8.1 of the Convention (the right to privacy) even though it was in accordance with the law. The court went on to consider issues arising under Article 8.2 which provide for the legitimate aims served by that law. The government had relied on "protection of morals" and "the protection of the rights of others" as legitimate aims under Article 8.2. The court stated that it "recognises that one of the purposes of the legislation is to afford safeguards for vulnerable members of society, such as the young, against the consequences of homosexual practices", and accepted that that was a legitimate aim. However, the court ruled that there could not be, in the circumstances, a "pressing social need" to make such acts criminal – that the interference, although in accordance with the law, and serving a legitimate aim, was disproportionate because there was no pressing social need. Whether a law prohibiting buggery between adult males and young boys would have been proportionate is an interesting question.

CARAF v UK

Christians Against Racism and Fascism v UK [1980] 21 DR 138 (CARAF) (see above, page 119) concerned an association of church organisations, community and race relations units and various other organisations whose aim was, *inter alia*, to generate public awareness of the dangers of racist and fascistic ideology, to promote racial justice and to oppose the divisive activities of the National Front and the National Party. CARAF had planned to hold a procession in the City of London on 22 April 1978 to promote the aims of the organisation. The march was considered to be necessary to counter the activities of groups with racist and fascist views which were gaining wide publicity. The organisation gave notice to the Metropolitan Police, although this was not a legal requirement.

The Metropolitan Police Commissioner imposed a ban on all marches and processions in London for two months beginning from 24 February 1978. He derived his authority for imposing the ban from s 3 of the Public Order Act 1936. The immediate effect of the order was to ban a march organised by the National Front which was to have taken place in Ilford on the 25 February 1978. Because the order ended on 24 April 1978 it also had the effect of banning the CARAF march.

CARAF complained to the ECHR that their Article 10 (expression) and Article 11 (peaceful assembly) rights, amongst others, were violated. The Commission said that, in this case, freedom of expression and freedom of peaceful assembly could not be separated. It went on to analyse the case in terms of Article 11 as that was the primary right which was engaged. There was no argument that the right had in fact been interfered with. Clearly it had.

Was the ban prescribed by law? The Commission looked at s 3 of the Public Order Act 1936 and said it had no doubt that the measure taken by the Metropolitan Police Commissioner on behalf of the government was in fact prescribed by law, as required by Article 11.2.

What were the legitimate aims pursued by the government in imposing the ban? The legitimate aims invoked by the government under Article 11.2 were the interests of public safety, the prevention of disorder or crime and the protection of the rights of others. The Commission accepted that the imposition of the ban was to prevent disorder. The Commission was influenced by the government's contention that there existed, at the time, in the UK, particular circumstances which required the government to act in the way it did; and that the lesser measures, short of a ban, available to the government under s 3, were not sufficient to prevent "serious public disorder". The Commission found that the ban had been imposed in pursuit of legitimate aims in Article 11.2.

Was the restriction or interference necessary in a democratic society? CARAF questioned the necessity in a democratic society of the use of the wide powers conferred on the Metropolitan Police Commissioner under the Public Order Act 1936. Further, they questioned the use of such powers in relation to the wholly peaceful protest that they had planned. The government argued that account must be taken of the tense atmosphere that existed in London at the time. There was a real fear that serious public disorder would result from the marches planned by the National Front.

The Commission accepted that the Public Order Act 1936 did not allow for arbitrary bans on particular demonstrations and applied evenly. It went on to say that a general ban on marches can be justified only if there is a serious danger of public disorder being occasioned which cannot be prevented by lesser means. The government must take into account the effect of the ban on peaceful marches which do not give rise to fears of public disorder and balance the competing interests. Only where the security considerations outweigh the interests of the marchers will the ban be regarded as necessary in a democratic society. The Commission was invited to examine the recent history of violence and public disorder that had resulted in the UK when marches by the National Front had been allowed.

In the circumstances the Commission held that it was not unreasonable for the government to have imposed the ban, and that the measures taken were proportionate to the legitimate aims pursued by the ban. It concluded that the ban, including its effect on CARAF's planned march, was justified as necessary in a democratic society within the meaning of Article 11.2. The application was ruled inadmissible.

Sunday Times v UK

In *Sunday Times v UK* [1979] 2 EHRR 245 a company had marketed thalidomide, which had been taken by a number of pregnant women who in due time gave birth to deformed babies. The women issued civil proceedings and were engaged in protracted negotiations without the case being tried. The *Sunday Times* newspaper began a series of articles aiming to assist the women to obtain a more generous settlement. One such article dealt with the way in which the drug had been tested, manufactured and eventually marketed. The Attorney-General, acting for the government, applied for and obtained an injunction prohibiting the publication of that article on the basis that to do so would be a contempt of court.

The *Sunday Times* and a group of journalists complained to Strasbourg that their Article 10 right to freedom of expression had been infringed.

The court subjected the petition to the analyses discussed above. Clearly, there had been a restriction or an interference with the Article 10 rights. Was it prescribed by law? If so, what was the legitimate aim that was being protected or invoked? Were the measures taken (the injunction) proportionate to the legitimate aim pursued? Was it necessary in a democratic society – was there a pressing social need?

The government argued that Article 10.2 allows for such restrictions and interference ". . . as are prescribed by law and are necessary in a democratic society . . . for maintaining the authority and impartiality of the judiciary".

Was the injunction prescribed by law? The newspaper and the journalists argued that the common law on contempt of court, at the time, did not meet the requirements of the Convention. As discussed above, the law must be adequately accessible and must be formulated with sufficient precision to allow a citizen to behave accordingly. The court examined the domestic law on contempt of court and said that a deliberate attempt to influence the settlement of pending proceedings was a contempt, and that the English law was sufficiently precise to enable the petitioners to foresee to a reasonable degree that their article might constitute a contempt. The court found that the restriction and interference with the petitioners' right of freedom of expression was "prescribed by law" in accordance with Article 10.2.

What was the legitimate aim pursued? The government maintained that the injunction was necessary "for maintaining the authority and impartiality of the judiciary". The judiciary includes the machinery of justice and the judicial arm of the government as well as the judges in their individual capacities. This legitimate aim recognises that the proper forum for determining disputes is the courts. The public should have respect for and confidence in the courts' ability to fulfil that role, the maintenance of which was one of the functions of the contempt laws. The court went on to find that the article did offend the rules on contempt of court, and that the action taken fell within the legitimate aim of maintaining the authority of the judiciary, and so the injunction against publication of the article by the *Sunday Times* newspaper was an interference that had a legitimate aim under Article 10.2.

Was the restriction or interference proportionate to the legitimate aim pursued? Was the interference necessary in a democratic society – was there a pressing social need for the interference? The publication of the proposed article would not have added any more pressure on the company to settle on better terms. The proposed article ". . . was couched in moderate terms and did not just present one side of the evidence, its publication would not have had adverse consequences for the 'authority of the judiciary'." It is true, said the ECHR, that the domestic courts are the proper forum for resolving disputes but this does not prohibit prior discussion. It is the function of the press and the media to impart information and ideas on matters that are of legal interest just as in other areas of public life. The thalidomide disaster was a matter of public concern and Article 10 guaranteed not only the freedom of the press, but also the right of the public to be informed. The families had a vital interest in knowing all the underlying facts which could assist them in their claim against the company. The court found that:

> "In view of all the circumstances, the interference did not correspond to a social need sufficiently pressing to outweigh the public interest in freedom of expression; the reasons for the restraint were not therefore sufficient under Article 10.2; it was not pro-

portionate to the legitimate aim pursued; and it was not necessary in a democratic society for maintaining the authority of the judiciary. Accordingly, Article 10 had been breached."

Thus, the ECHR's approach to analysing the Convention rights can be summarised as follows:

- Any restriction or interference must be in accordance with the law or prescribed by law – there must be some basis in national law which must be adequately accessible and sufficiently precise.
- The restriction or interference must be justified by one of the legitimate aims recognised under the Convention and its articles.
- The restriction or interference must be proportionate to the legitimate aim pursued – was it necessary in a democratic society?
- The restriction or interference must not be applied in a discriminatory fashion.

"Necessary in a democratic society" means that the restriction or interference must:

- fulfil a pressing social need, and
- pursue a legitimate aim, and
- there must be proportionality between the means adopted and the legitimate aims.

Margin of Appreciation

The doctrine of margin of appreciation is an important principle of interpretation adopted by the ECHR. It allows a member state a degree of flexibility and freedom to assess its public policy decisions although subject to review by the ECHR. This recognises that the ECHR has to be sensitive to and respect the member states' political and cultural traditions – the "subsidiarity" principle. What may offend religious and other sensibilities in one country may be seen as free speech in another.

Sometimes, therefore, in determining whether a social policy aim is legitimate or the means used to achieve it are necessary in a democratic society, the ECHR recognises limits to its own competence to judge the issue. It does this by allowing the state "a margin of appreciation" in assessing an alleged violation. A broader margin of appreciation is allowed in cases involving an assessment of national security or public morality.

Handyside v UK [1976] 1 EHRR 737 concerned a book called *The*

Little Red Schoolbook. It had been published for school children and contained a section on sex. The books were seized under the Obscene Publications Act 1959, and an application for forfeiture had been made after the publishers had been convicted and fined. The ECHR had to decide whether such interference was necessary in a democratic society for the protection of morals under Article 10.2, the petitioner having invoked Article 10.1 – freedom of expression. The court stated:

> "In particular it is not possible to find in the domestic law of the various Contracting States a uniform European conception of morals. The view taken by their respective laws of the requirements of morals varies from time to time and from place to place, especially in our era which is characterised by a rapid and far-reaching evolution of opinions on the subject. By reason of their direct and continuous contact with the vital forces of their countries, State authorities are in a better position than the international judge to give an opinion upon the exact contents of these requirements as well as on the 'necessity' of a 'restriction' or 'penalty' intended to meet them . . . Consequently, Article 10.2 leaves to the Contracting states a margin of appreciation . . ."

The court went on to add that Article 10 does not give the Contracting States an unlimited power of appreciation. The domestic margin of appreciation thus goes hand in hand with European supervision.

In numerous other cases the ECHR has allowed, and indeed has said that States are allowed, a margin to take into account domestic circumstances and social policy. In the *CARAF* case Strasbourg was not prepared to interfere with the assessment made by the domestic authorities as to the tense and serious public order situation that existed. It said:

> "The government, . . . invoking the margin of appreciation permitted to the High Contracting Parties by the . . . provision of the Convention, consider the measures taken as necessary. In their view, regard must be had to the tense atmosphere prevailing in London at the relevant time. . ."

The general approach to the margin of appreciation is to allow a greater margin in issues of public morality, as in the case of *Handyside,* and national security, as in the *CARAF* case. It is for the national authorities to make the initial assessment as to necessity and pressing social need in each case, and the states are afforded that margin. However, the decision of the state is subject to Strasbourg supervision. So in the *Dudgeon* case, which involved an assessment of morality – and one would have thought a margin would have been allowed in accordance with its judgment in *Handyside* – the ECHR felt it had to intervene in the domestic assessment of the necessity and pressing social need for the law prohibiting buggery between consenting adult males in Northern Ireland. The court exercised its supervisory role even though morality is an area where a margin would be allowed to the domestic authorities. It looks not only at the nature of the aim pursued but also at the nature of the activities involved, which will affect the scope of the margin of appreciation. In the *Dudgeon* case the activities concerned a most intimate aspect of private life.

In the *Sunday Times* case, the ECHR said that Article 10.2 did leave to states a margin of appreciation to interpret and apply the law in force, but the exercise of that margin was not unlimited. The final say on whether the restriction or interference was consistent with Article 10.2 remained with Strasbourg. This supervision was not limited to determining whether the exercise of the discretion by the domestic authority was reasonable. The ambit and scope of the domestic margin of appreciation was not the same in respect of all the legitimate aims in Article 10.2. Domestic authorities are in a better position to determine the "protection of public morals", but the same margin may not be available in the "far more objective" aim of "the authority of the judiciary", resulting in greater ECHR supervision and correspondingly lesser margin of appreciation.

Derogations

Article 15 of the Convention allows governments to derogate from their obligations under the Convention during "war or other public emergency threatening the life of the nation". This permits the state to restrict the exercise of some of the rights and freedoms without violating the Convention. Any derogation must be proportional. Section 1(2) of the Human Rights Act 1998 allows the government to avoid incorporating that part of the Convention in relation to which a derogation has been entered.

The current derogation in place (see Part I of Sched 3 to the Act) allows the police to detain a person under the Prevention of Terrorism (Temporary Provisions) Act 1984 for up to seven days. In *Brogan v UK* [1988] 11 EHRR 117 the Strasbourg court had held that periods of detention of longer than four days without production before a court "promptly" as required by Article 5.3 was a violation of that article. In recognition of the emergency in Northern Ireland, instead of changing the law to reflect the *Brogan* judgment, the UK entered a derogation pursuant to Article 15 of the Convention. This derogation was unsuccessfully challenged in *Branningan v UK* [1993] 17 EHRR 539. See also page 123.

Reservations
Parties to the Convention may also enter certain reservations to their agreement to be bound by the Convention. There is currently in force one reservation by the UK (see Part II of Sched 3 to the Act). The second sentence of Article 2 of the First Protocol (requiring education to be provided in conformity with parent's religious and philosophical convictions) has been accepted only in so far as it is compatible with the provision of efficient instruction and training and the avoidance of unreasonable public expenditure. See also page 125.

Article 13
Article 13, concerning effective remedies for breach of Convention rights, proved controversial during the passage of the Human Rights Act 1998 and the government decided not to incorporate this article. It provides:
   "Everyone whose rights and freedoms as set forth in this Convention are violated shall have an effective remedy before a national authority notwithstanding that the violation has been committed by persons acting in an official capacity."
The government argued that Article 13 was not necessary because s 8 of the Act itself provides sufficient procedures and remedies for the enforcement of the Convention rights. The government feared that the inclusion of Article 13 would cause, and indeed encourage, unwarranted judicial activity in the field of damages and compensation. The Home Secretary (Jack Straw), for example, said that the inclusion of Article 13 would cause confusion or that it would lead the courts to act in ways not intended by the Act, by creating remedies going beyond those created by s 8: "In considering Article 13 the courts could decide to grant damages in more circumstances than we had envisaged". (*Hansard*, HC, 20 May 1996).
   The Lord Chancellor, Lord Irvine of Lairg, in the House of Lords

Committee Stage (*Hansard* HL, 18 November 1998, col 475), said that the Convention rights can be raised in domestic courts and remedies are provided in s 8:

> "If the concern is to ensure that the [Act] provides an exhaustive code of remedies for those whose Convention rights have been violated, we believe that [s 8] already achieves that and that nothing further is needed. We have set out in the [Act] to provide remedies for violations of Convention rights and we do not believe that it is necessary to add to it . . ."

He went on to say that it might lead the courts to fashion remedies other than s 8 remedies, which are sufficient and clear:

> "We believe that [s 8] provides effective remedies before our courts . . . to incorporate expressly Article 13 may lead to courts fashioning remedies about which we know nothing other than [s 8] remedies which we regard as sufficient and clear."

The government was concerned that the courts would create fresh remedies where none existed before. The intention is to give effect to Convention rights within the existing extensive regime of remedies. This remains, perhaps, one of the most fascinating aspects of the Act. Will the courts adhere to the established domestic legal philosophy of not punishing the executive for wrongs in ways which fall outside the traditional methods, or will they want to create new remedies, such as ruling inadmissible evidence obtained in breach of a Convention right, for instance, Article 8. Will the courts give reduced sentences, as a remedy, for a breach of a Convention right? Lord Nolan, in the House of Lords, in the case of *Khan (Sultan)* (see page 101), said that evidence so obtained was admissible (this issue was a matter for the domestic courts). He observed that he had reached that decision not only as a matter of law,

> ". . . but also with relief. It would be a strange reflection on our law that evidence should be excluded in a case where a defendant had admitted his part in large scale drug importation because his right to privacy had been invaded."

It would be stranger still if his sentence was reduced on the same grounds having admitted the evidence. This surely could not have been the intention of Parliament in passing this momentous Act! Neither the Act nor the Convention lay down a rule of exclusion. Admissibility, so say Strasbourg repeatedly, is a matter for regulation for national courts. In jurisdictions where evidence is excluded if obtained in breach of human rights legislation there are specific domestic rules which govern such admissibility or exclusion. The regime for receiving human rights provisions in the UK domestic system are wholly different.

Section 2 of the Act obliges the courts to have regard to ECHR jurisprudence when a question arises under the Act "in connection with" a Convention right. Article 13 plays an important role in the Convention and Strasbourg jurisprudence. It seems, therefore, that the domestic courts will be able to have regard to Article 13 and the jurisprudence founded upon it.

This may be important in certain circumstances and in some cases. In *Chahal v UK* [1996] 23 EHRR 413 the right to an effective remedy was crucial to the judgment of the court. The case concerned the detention and threatened deportation of a Sikh activist; the government said he was a terrorist and that there was a danger to national security. The key question was whether the national courts could provide an effective remedy, given that, for reasons of protecting national security, no details of the case against him could be given. The ECHR decided that there was no effective remedy. As a result of this case the government enacted the Special Immigration Appeals Commission Act 1998, which creates a new and special right of appeal in such cases.

Checklist
- The ECHR adopts an analytical approach.
- The rule of law – legitimacy.
- Legitimate aims.
- Proportionality.
- "Necessary in a democratic society".
- Means – is there a pressing social need?
- Non-discrimination.
- Margin of appreciation, but subject to ECHR supervision.
- Greater margin allowed for particular types of legitimate aim; even so, the ECHR examines the nature of the right involved, the extent of the interference and the aim pursued.
- Derogations.
- Reservations.
- Article 13 (remedies): reasons for exclusion.

Chapter 7

Enforcing the Convention Rights

Public Authorities

The Convention rights made available in UK law by the Human Rights Act 1998 are enforceable against "public authorities". Section 6 creates a statutory cause of action against them.

Section 6(1) of the Act makes it unlawful for a public authority to act in a way which is incompatible with a Convention right. One purpose of the Act is to preserve the doctrine of parliamentary legislative supremacy (see page 47) and so s 6(2) says that s 6(1) does not apply to a public authority which is acting in accordance with its statutory duty; could not have acted any differently; and was prevented by a statutory duty from acting in conformity with the Convention. The position is the same where the public authority is acting under a duty arising from subordinate legislation. In such circumstances the courts identified in s 4(5) can make "declarations of incompatibility". However, as has been seen, the interpretative obligation requires the court to interpret the provision in a way which permits the public authority to give effect to the Convention if such a meaning is possible.

Section 6(3) defines a "public authority" as:
- a court or tribunal, and
- any person certain of whose functions are of a public nature but does not include either House of Parliament (although it does include the House of Lords in its judicial capacity).

A person is not a public authority if the nature of the act is private.

There are some bodies which are obviously "full-blooded" public authorities. Examples of these are courts or tribunals, the police, government departments, and prisons. Any body, although not an obviously and full-blooded public authority, certain of whose functions are public in nature, will qualify as a public authority. An example given by the Lord Chancellor is Railtrack, one of whose functions is in relation to public safety on the railways. Acts or omissions carried out in this respect will be acts of a public authority, but acts carried out in its capacity as a private property developer, for example, will not.

The effect of s 6 is that if a public authority infringes a Convention right it will be possible to invoke the Act against it:

- as a ground for judicial review on the basis of illegality (breach of s 6(1) of the Act);
- to bring private law proceedings against it for breach of statutory duty; or
- to use the public body's illegal action as a defence in any proceedings it may bring itself.

The Limitation Period

Section 7(5) establishes that cases against public authorities alleging a breach of the Convention must be brought within one year beginning with the date the alleged breach takes place. This is subject to an extension where the court considers it to be equitable in all the circumstances. The normal time limit is subject to any rule which imposes a stricter time limit in relation to the proceedings in question (for example, the three-months time limit for bringing proceedings by way of judicial review).

Standing

Under s 7(1) and (3) of the Act, proceedings may be brought only by a person who is, or would be, a victim of a violation, even if the person would have sufficient standing to be a party to judicial review proceedings on the broader test of "standing" under the Rules of Supreme Court, Order 53.

Under s 7(7) only a victim or would-be victim can bring an action for judicial review in relation to unlawful acts. A victim for this purpose is a victim only if he would be a victim for the purpose of Article 34 of the Convention if proceedings were brought in the ECHR.

Remedies

Declarations of Incompatibility

Where the interpretative obligation has failed to produce an interpretation compatible with the Convention rights, then, although the court must give primacy to the domestic statute, the higher courts have the power to make "declarations of incompatibility" under s 4(2) of the Human Rights Act 1998.

Such a declaration will generate public interest and pressure on the government will be to change the law. However, the courts are unlikely to want to engage in making such declarations. They will prefer to seek meanings to statutory provisions which conform with the Convention.

The power to make declarations is available only in the courts listed in s 4(5) of the Act. Although the Convention can be argued, and should be argued, where a Convention point is taken, the lower courts must interpret primary legislation compatibly with the Convention, so far as is possible. Declarations of incompatibility are not available in the county court, tribunals (except employment appeal tribunals), Crown Courts or magistrates' courts.

Where a compatible interpretation is not possible in the lower courts they must follow the legislation and respect the important constitutional principle of parliamentary legislative supremacy. To reach a decision the lower court would sometimes need to take a view of the Convention issues if raised and relevant, and their effect in the proceedings before it. They may do this when stating a case for the purpose of an appeal from a magistrates' court, and would have to set out their views about the Convention and the legislation, and whether they are compatible. Any such view by the lower courts will not trigger the remedial order procedure in s 10 of the Human Rights Act 1998. It will, however, begin a process of creating pressure to remedy legislation which offends against the Convention.

Even though the s 4(5) courts can make a declaration of incompatibility they do not have the power to set aside an incompatible domestic statute: s 3(2)(b) and (c). The declaration triggers the s 10 remedial order procedure ("fast track") for the amendment of legislation which has been deemed to be incompatible with a Convention right. Similarly, an adverse ECHR judgment alone will not operate to invalidate domestic legislation. But pressure on the government will begin. An adverse judgment may trigger (not automatically, but on a political will) the s 10 remedial order or "fast track" procedure.

Professor A T H Smith in *The Human Rights Act and the Criminal Lawyer - The Constitutional Context* [1999] CLR 251 at 259 says:

". . . the upshot is that the applicant has established that he ought to have won his case, because his rights have been infringed, but he loses since the declaration does not actually affect the outcome of the proceedings in question".

There may be a costs implication for a litigant whose "benefit" may simply be the possibility of a "declaration of incompatibility". The Legal Aid Act requirement to show a "reasonable prospect of success" may not be satisfied unless "success" is given a wide meaning. The consequence of a declaration is not the conclusion of proceedings in favour of the applicant whose rights were infringed. The Act states in s 4(6)(b) that a declaration is not binding on the parties to the proceedings in which it is made. This allows the government to take a different position from that of the court. Where this occurs the matter would be resolved in the ECHR. Where a domestic court is considering whether to make a declaration the government is entitled to notice under s 5 and to be joined as a party in the proceedings. The Crown is allowed a particular right of appeal under s 5(4), with leave, to the House of Lords against any declaration of incompatibility made in criminal proceedings.

The "Fast Track" Procedure

The fast track procedure is activated once a declaration has been made by a s 4(5) court or where, as a result of a decision of the ECHR, it appears to the government that a change in the law is required. Section 10 of the Act allows the Minister responsible to make a "remedial order" which must be in the form of a statutory instrument amending the legislation so as to correct the incompatibility. There is a standard and an emergency procedure (Sched 2, paragraph 2(a) and (b)).

The Standard Procedure

The standard procedure requires an order with the "required information" to be laid before Parliament for 60 days. Representations can be made and amendments allowed. If so, details of the representations and any amendments must be laid before Parliament again. The order does not come into force unless it is approved by both Houses of Parliament by resolution within 60 days after it is laid the second time.

The Emergency Procedure

Under the emergency procedure pursuant to Sched 2, paragraph 2(b) the government (Minister) may make the Order before laying it before Parliament, but must state that in his/her opinion, because of the emergency, it is necessary to make the Order without Parliamentary approval. The Order is then laid before Parliament, with the required information, for 60 days. Representations can be made and if appropriate amendments can be made, as under the standard procedure. Whether or not amendments have been made the Order must be laid before Parliament again, with a summary of any representations and details of any amendments. It will cease to have effect 120 days after it was made unless it is approved by a resolution by both Houses.

The power to act under s 10 applies to both primary and secondary legislation. This provision will, in practice, allow interest groups and lobbyists to make representations following any case in the ECHR or any declaration of incompatibility by the domestic courts. The government is not bound to act following a declaration, although the overwhelming expectation is that it will.

Effect of a Remedial Order

The remedial order can be wide in scope and can have retrospective effect. The retrospective effect is, however, limited by Sched 2, paragraph 1(4), which states that no person will be held to be guilty of an offence as a result of the retrospective effect of the remedial order. It seems, therefore, that the remedial order procedure can be used to backdate changes required as a result of a declaration by the domestic courts or an adverse ECHR judgment.

Unlawful Acts of Public Authorities

Section 6 introduces a vital strand of the Act, which entitles an individual to take proceedings asserting or defending Convention rights.

Where a provision or provisions of primary legislation cannot be read so as to be compatible with the Convention, then if a public authority acted in accordance with that provision(s), and could not have acted any differently, the act cannot be unlawful as the authority was acting in accordance with its statutory duty. This is the general effect of s 6(2).

Section 6 protects any public authority acting in accordance with primary legislation, but only if the authority could not have acted any differently, ie, had no choice but to act in the way it did. Similarly, s 6(2)(b) protects public authorities who are enforcing provisions which are, or are derived from, primary legislation even if the provisions are incompatible with the Convention rights. It will be recalled that s 4(6) provides that a declaration of incompatibility does not affect the validity, continuing operation or enforcement of domestic provisions.

"Public authority" does not include either House of Parliament, but does include the House of Lords in its judicial capacity: s 6(3) and (4). Thus failure to put before Parliament a proposal for legislation, or failure to make any primary legislation or remedial order, will not be unlawful and cannot be challenged. This is to protect parliamentary legislative supremacy. Likewise, a Minister's failure to make a remedial order following a declaration cannot be challenged.

Section 7 provides individuals with direct access to bring proceedings under s 7(1)(a) in respect of the acts of public authorities. This is a key enabling section for individuals who claim that such an authority has acted, or proposes to act, contrary to s 6(1), i.e. in a manner which is not compatible with a Convention right, permitting them to bring proceedings against that authority in the appropriate court or tribunal, or rely on the Convention right in any legal proceedings: s 7(1)(a) and (b).

Thus, individuals are intended to benefit in a number of ways. Most significantly, they may rely on their Convention rights not only in proceedings which they bring under s 7(1)(a), but also in any proceedings, so long as they are victims, or potential victims, of an unlawful act of a public authority: s 7(1)(b). Furthermore, an important link is provided by the requirement that all courts and tribunals, so far as possible, read and give effect to primary and secondary legislation in a way which is compatible with the Convention rights (s 3), whether or not a party is a victim, or a potential victim, of a public authority. It is submitted that many Convention points will be taken and tested in proceedings brought other than under s 7(1)(a).

Only a victim or a potential victim of an unlawful act of a public authority may sue. A victim for the purposes of this section is the same as that under Article 34 of the Convention: s 7(7). Article 34 states:

"any person, non-governmental organisation or group of individuals claiming to be the victim of a violation . . . may make a complaint under the Convention."

There is extensive body of case law on who is a victim. It is important to note that the definition does not include those who have "sufficient interest" as in domestic public law: s 31(3), Supreme Court Act 1981 and the Rules of Supreme Court, Order 53. Interest groups are also excluded.

Section 7(3) provides that a person bringing proceedings under the Act by way of judicial review will be taken to have a sufficient interest in relation to the unlawful act only if he is, or would be, a victim of that act. It is, therefore, clear that an individual will not escape the "victim" test by bringing the action under the Rules of the Supreme Court, Order 53, rule 3(7).

Rules will be made determining the "appropriate court or tribunal" and the Minister responsible may add to the relief or remedies the court may grant and the grounds upon which to make them, so that it can provide appropriate remedies in respect of unlawful act: s 7(2), (9) and (11).

A person bringing proceedings under s 7(3) by way of judicial review is not given the same time within which to bring proceedings as is a person bringing an application under s 7(1)(a) in the designated "appropriate court or tribunal". The judicial review litigant remains subject to Order 53 rule 4, which requires the applicant to bring proceedings "promptly and in any event within three months". The litigant in the "appropriate court or tribunal" may apply within one year of the act complained of or within such longer period as the court thinks equitable: s 7(5). In effect, therefore, the applicant opts for one or other time limit.

Section 7(8) states that "nothing in this Act creates a criminal offence". The Act is not intended to impose any criminal liability on any public authority in respect of its unlawful acts. Of course, if the unlawful act complained of amounts to a criminal offence it can be dealt with in the usual way.

Under s 8(1) of the Act the court or tribunal can "grant such relief or remedy, or make such order, within its power as it considers just and appropriate". By virtue of s 8(2), however, damages will be awarded only if that court or tribunal has the power to award damages or compensation in civil proceedings. This power to grant relief is not restricted to actions brought under s 7(1)(a) but may be exercised in any proceedings (within the powers of the court or tribunal) in which a Convention right is relied upon.

Damages and compensation are to be awarded after all the circumstances are taken into account. The court or tribunal will consider any other relief and the consequences of any decisions in respect of the unlawful act. Damages and compensation will be awarded only if the court is satisfied that the award is necessary to afford "just satisfaction". The courts are obliged to take into account the ECHR jurisprudence and the principles applied by the ECHR under Article 41 in determining whether or not to make an award, and if so, the level of the award. The jurisprudence under Article 41 indicates that the level of awards is unlikely to be as high as in some domestic courts.

An action under s 7(1)(a) in respect of "judicial acts" can be brought only by exercising a right of appeal, or by way of judicial review (or in a forum prescribed by rules). This is the general effect of s 9(1) and (5).

"Judicial acts" means acts of a court or tribunal, or of a judge or a person acting on behalf or on the instructions of a judge, or tribunal member, Justice of the Peace or Clerk or officer entitled to exercise the jurisdiction of the court or tribunal.

Section 9 prevents applicants from applying to the "appropriate court or tribunal" established to hear applications under s 7(1) unless such a course is later prescribed by rules. This forces applicants to stay within the process in which the unlawful act is said to have occurred, and restricts them to the procedures and time limits set down in that process or procedure. Judicial acts complained of arising on a trial on indictment will have to be appealed against or judicially reviewed in the usual way providing there is no rule prohibiting judicial review. It is unlikely that a defendant in a criminal case will be allowed to leave the criminal jurisdiction under the "appropriate court or tribunal" rule. This would cause untold delay in the administration of criminal cases. The House of Lords, perhaps, had this concern in mind in the case of *R v Director of Public Prosecutions, Ex parte Kebilene and Others*, [1999] WLR 972, in refusing to accept that a possible Convention issue in a trial on indictment could be subjected to "collateral challenges", thereby causing delay to the indictment.

Section 9 does not affect any rule of law which prevents a court from being the subject of judicial review: s 9(2). Certain issues arising on a trial on indictment cannot be subject to judicial review.

Section 9(3) prevents the award of damages and compensation for "judicial acts" done in good faith, except for the purposes of Article 5.5 which states that everyone who has been a victim of arrest or detention in contravention of the provisions of that article shall have an enforceable right to compensation.

The award is made against the Crown after a Minister is joined as a party: s 9(4).

Checklist

Public Authorities
- Meaning of public authority.
- Duty to act compatibly.
- Protection under s 6(2).
- Actions under s 7.
- Time limits depend on the path chosen.
- Damages and compensation under s 8, but power only in those courts which are empowered to award damages.
- No damages or compensation for judicial acts done in good faith.
- Specific retention of right to damages or compensation for violations of Article 55..

Remedies
- Declarations of incompatibility.
- Incompatibility does not invalidate domestic law (parliamentary legislative supremacy).
- May trigger the "fast track" procedure.
- Adverse Strasbourg judgment.
- Domestic law not invalidated by declaration of incompatibility (parliamentary legislative supremacy).
- The "fast track" procedure.
- Unlawful acts of public authorities.
- ECHR can award "just satisfaction"; this could include compensation, damages, costs, expenses.
- Often only costs and expenses are allowed as just satisfaction even though a violation may be found.

Appendix 1

The Human Rights Act 1998

Arrangement of Sections

22. Short title, commencement, application and extent

Schedules

An Act to give further effect to rights and freedoms guaranteed under the European Convention on Human Rights; to make provision with respect to holders of certain judicial offices who become judges of the European Court of Human Rights; and for connected purposes.
[9th November 1998]

BE IT ENACTED by the Queen's most Excellent Majesty, by and with the advice and consent of the Lords Spiritual and Temporal, and Commons, in this present Parliament assembled, and by the authority of the same, as follows:–

Introduction
The Convention Rights
1. – (1) In this Act "the Convention rights" means the rights and fundamental freedoms set out in–
      (a) Articles 2 to 12 and 14 of the Convention,
      (b) Articles 1 to 3 of the First Protocol, and
      (c) Articles 1 and 2 of the Sixth Protocol,
as read with Articles 16 to 18 of the Convention.

    (2) Those Articles are to have effect for the purposes of this Act subject to any designated derogation or reservation (as to which see sections 14 and 15).

    (3) The Articles are set out in Schedule 1.

    (4) The Secretary of State may by order make such amendments to this Act as he considers appropriate to reflect the effect, in relation to the United Kingdom, of a protocol.

    (5) In subsection (4) "protocol" means a protocol to the Convention–
      (a) which the United Kingdom has ratified; or
      (b) which the United Kingdom has signed with a view to ratification.

    (6) No amendment may be made by an order under subsection (4) so as to come into force before the protocol concerned is in force in relation to the

United Kingdom.

Interpretation of Convention rights

2. – (1) A court or tribunal determining a question which has arisen in connection with a Convention right must take into account any–

    (a) judgment, decision, declaration or advisory opinion of the European Court of Human Rights,

    (b) opinion of the Commission given in a report adopted under Article 31 of the Convention,

    (c) decision of the Commission in connection with Article 26 or 27(2) of the Convention, or

    (d) decision of the Committee of Ministers taken under Article 46 of the Convention,

whenever made or given, so far as, in the opinion of the court or tribunal, it is relevant to the proceedings in which that question has arisen.

    (2) Evidence of any judgment, decision, declaration or opinion of which account may have to be taken under this section is to be given in proceedings before any court or tribunal in such manner as may be provided by rules.

    (3) In this section "rules" means rules of court or, in the case of proceedings before a tribunal, rules made for the purposes of this section–

    (a) by the Lord Chancellor or the Secretary of State, in relation to any proceedings outside Scotland;

    (b) by the Secretary of State, in relation to proceedings in Scotland; or

    (c) by a Northern Ireland department, in relation to proceedings before a tribunal in Northern Ireland–

        (i) which deals with transferred matters; and

        (ii) for which no rules made under paragraph (a) are in force.

Legislation

Interpretation of legislation

3. – (1) So far as it is possible to do so, primary legislation and subordinate legislation must be read and given effect in a way which is compatible with the Convention rights.

    (2) This section–

    (a) applies to primary legislation and subordinate legislation whenever enacted;

    (b) does not affect the validity, continuing operation or enforcement of any incompatible primary legislation; and

    (c) does not affect the validity, continuing operation or enforcement of any incompatible subordinate legislation if (disregarding any possibility of revocation) primary legislation prevents removal of the incompatibility.

Declaration of incompatibility

4. – (1) Subsection (2) applies in any proceedings in which a court determines whether a provision of primary legislation is compatible with a Convention right.

(2) If the court is satisfied that the provision is incompatible with a Convention right, it may make a declaration of that incompatibility.

(3) Subsection (4) applies in any proceedings in which a court determines whether a provision of subordinate legislation, made in the exercise of a power conferred by primary legislation, is compatible with a Convention right.

(4) If the court is satisfied–

(a) that the provision is incompatible with a Convention right, and

(b) that (disregarding any possibility of revocation) the primary legislation concerned prevents removal of the incompatibility,

it may make a declaration of that incompatibility.

(5) In this section "court" means–

(a) the House of Lords;

(b) the Judicial Committee of the Privy Council;

(c) the Courts-Martial Appeal Court;

(d) in Scotland, the High Court of Justiciary sitting otherwise than as a trial court or the Court of Session;

(e) in England and Wales or Northern Ireland, the High Court or the Court of Appeal.

(6) A declaration under this section ("a declaration of incompatibility")–

(a) does not affect the validity, continuing operation or enforcement of the provision in respect of which it is given; and

(b) is not binding on the parties to the proceedings in which it is made.

Right of Crown to intervene

5. – (1) Where a court is considering whether to make a declaration of incompatibility, the Crown is entitled to notice in accordance with rules of court.

(2) In any case to which subsection (1) applies–

(a) a Minister of the Crown (or a person nominated by him),

(b) a member of the Scottish Executive,

(c) a Northern Ireland Minister,

(d) a Northern Ireland department,

is entitled, on giving notice in accordance with rules of court, to be joined as a party to the proceedings.

(3) Notice under subsection (2) may be given at any time during the proceedings.

(4) A person who has been made a party to criminal proceedings (other

than in Scotland) as the result of a notice under subsection (2) may, with leave, appeal to the House of Lords against any declaration of incompatibility made in the proceedings.

(5) In subsection (4)–

"criminal proceedings" includes all proceedings before the Courts-Martial Appeal Court; and

"leave" means leave granted by the court making the declaration of incompatibility or by the House of Lords.

Public authorities
Acts of public authorities

6. –(1) It is unlawful for a public authority to act in a way which is incompatible with a Convention right.

(2) Subsection (1) does not apply to an act if–

(a) as the result of one or more provisions of primary legislation, the authority could not have acted differently; or

(b) in the case of one or more provisions of, or made under, primary legislation which cannot be read or given effect in a way which is compatible with the Convention rights, the authority was acting so as to give effect to or enforce those provisions.

(3) In this section "public authority" includes–

(a) a court or tribunal, and

(b) any person certain of whose functions are functions of a public nature,

but does not include either House of Parliament or a person exercising functions in connection with proceedings in Parliament.

(4) In subsection (3) "Parliament" does not include the House of Lords in its judicial capacity.

(5) In relation to a particular act, a person is not a public authority by virtue only of subsection (3)(b) if the nature of the act is private.

(6) "An act" includes a failure to act but does not include a failure to–

(a) introduce in, or lay before, Parliament a proposal for legislation; or

(b) make any primary legislation or remedial order.

Proceedings

7. – (1) A person who claims that a public authority has acted (or proposes to act) in a way which is made unlawful by section 6(1) may–

(a) bring proceedings against the authority under this Act in the appropriate court or tribunal, or

(b) rely on the Convention right or rights concerned in any legal proceedings,

but only if he is (or would be) a victim of the unlawful act.

(2) In subsection (1)(a) "appropriate court or tribunal" means such

court or tribunal as may be determined in accordance with rules; and proceedings against an authority include a counterclaim or similar proceeding.

(3) If the proceedings are brought on an application for judicial review, the applicant is to be taken to have a sufficient interest in relation to the unlawful act only if he is, or would be, a victim of that act.

(4) If the proceedings are made by way of a petition for judicial review in Scotland, the applicant shall be taken to have title and interest to sue in relation to the unlawful act only if he is, or would be, a victim of that act.

(5) Proceedings under subsection (1)(a) must be brought before the end of–

    (a) the period of one year beginning with the date on which the act complained of took place; or

    (b) such longer period as the court or tribunal considers equitable having regard to all the circumstances,

but that is subject to any rule imposing a stricter time limit in relation to the procedure in question.

(6) In subsection (1)(b) "legal proceedings" includes–

    (a) proceedings brought by or at the instigation of a public authority; and

    (b) an appeal against the decision of a court or tribunal.

(7) For the purposes of this section, a person is a victim of an unlawful act only if he would be a victim for the purposes of Article 34 of the Convention if proceedings were brought in the European Court of Human Rights in respect of that act.

(8) Nothing in this Act creates a criminal offence.

(9) In this section "rules" means–

    (a) in relation to proceedings before a court or tribunal outside Scotland, rules made by the Lord Chancellor or the Secretary of State for the purposes of this section or rules of court,

    (b) in relation to proceedings before a court or tribunal in Scotland, rules made by the Secretary of State for those purposes,

    (c) in relation to proceedings before a tribunal in Northern Ireland–

      (i) which deals with transferred matters; and

      (ii) for which no rules made under paragraph (a) are in force, rules made by a Northern Ireland department for those purposes,

and includes provision made by order under section 1 of the Courts and Legal Services Act 1990.

(10) In making rules, regard must be had to section 9.

(11) The Minister who has power to make rules in relation to a particular tribunal may, to the extent he considers it necessary to ensure that the tribunal can provide an appropriate remedy in relation to an act (or proposed act) of a public authority which is (or would be) unlawful as a result of sec-

tion 6(1), by order add to–
> (a) the relief or remedies which the tribunal may grant; or
> (b) the grounds on which it may grant any of them.

(12) An order made under subsection (11) may contain such incidental, supplemental, consequential or transitional provision as the Minister making it considers appropriate.

(13) "The Minister" includes the Northern Ireland department concerned.

Judicial remedies

8. – (1) In relation to any act (or proposed act) of a public authority which the court finds is (or would be) unlawful, it may grant such relief or remedy, or make such order, within its powers as it considers just and appropriate.

(2) But damages may be awarded only by a court which has power to award damages, or to order the payment of compensation, in civil proceedings.

(3) No award of damages is to be made unless, taking account of all the circumstances of the case, including–
> (a) any other relief or remedy granted, or order made, in relation to the act in question (by that or any other court), and
> (b) the consequences of any decision (of that or any other court) in respect of that act,

the court is satisfied that the award is necessary to afford just satisfaction to the person in whose favour it is made.

(4) In determining–
> (a) whether to award damages, or
> (b) the amount of an award,

the court must take into account the principles applied by the European Court of Human Rights in relation to the award of compensation under Article 41 of the Convention.

(5) A public authority against which damages are awarded is to be treated–
> (a) in Scotland, for the purposes of section 3 of the Law Reform (Miscellaneous Provisions) (Scotland) Act 1940 as if the award were made in an action of damages in which the authority has been found liable in respect of loss or damage to the person to whom the award is made;
> (b) for the purposes of the Civil Liability (Contribution) Act 1978 as liable in respect of damage suffered by the person to whom the award is made.

(6) In this section–

"court" includes a tribunal;

"damages" means damages for an unlawful act of a public authority; and "unlawful" means unlawful under section 6(1).

Judicial acts

9. – (1) Proceedings under section 7(1)(a) in respect of a judicial act may be brought only—

> (a) by exercising a right of appeal;
> (b) on an application (in Scotland a petition) for judicial review; or
> (c) in such other forum as may be prescribed by rules.

(2) That does not affect any rule of law which prevents a court from being the subject of judicial review.

(3) In proceedings under this Act in respect of a judicial act done in good faith, damages may not be awarded otherwise than to compensate a person to the extent required by Article 5(5) of the Convention.

(4) An award of damages permitted by subsection (3) is to be made against the Crown; but no award may be made unless the appropriate person, if not a party to the proceedings, is joined.

(5) In this section–

"appropriate person" means the Minister responsible for the court concerned, or a person or government department nominated by him;

"court" includes a tribunal;

"judge" includes a member of a tribunal, a justice of the peace and a clerk or other officer entitled to exercise the jurisdiction of a court;

"judicial act" means a judicial act of a court and includes an act done on the instructions, or on behalf, of a judge; and

"rules" has the same meaning as in section 7(9).

Remedial action

Power to take remedial action

10. – (1) This section applies if–

> (a) a provision of legislation has been declared under section 4 to be incompatible with a Convention right and, if an appeal lies–
>   (i) all persons who may appeal have stated in writing that they do not intend to do so;
>   (ii) the time for bringing an appeal has expired and no appeal has been brought within that time; or
>   (iii) an appeal brought within that time has been determined or abandoned; or
> (b) it appears to a Minister of the Crown or Her Majesty in Council that, having regard to a finding of the European Court of Human Rights made after the coming into force of this section in proceedings against the United Kingdom, a provision of legislation is incompatible with an obligation of the United Kingdom arising from the Convention.

(2) If a Minister of the Crown considers that there are compelling rea-

sons for proceeding under this section, he may by order make such amendments to the legislation as he considers necessary to remove the incompatibility.

(3) If, in the case of subordinate legislation, a Minister of the Crown considers–

> (a) that it is necessary to amend the primary legislation under which the subordinate legislation in question was made, in order to enable the incompatibility to be removed, and
>
> (b) that there are compelling reasons for proceeding under this section,

he may by order make such amendments to the primary legislation as he considers necessary.

(4) This section also applies where the provision in question is in subordinate legislation and has been quashed, or declared invalid, by reason of incompatibility with a Convention right and the Minister proposes to proceed under paragraph 2(b) of Schedule 2.

(5) If the legislation is an Order in Council, the power conferred by subsection (2) or (3) is exercisable by Her Majesty in Council.

(6) In this section "legislation" does not include a Measure of the Church Assembly or of the General Synod of the Church of England.

(7) Schedule 2 makes further provision about remedial orders.

Other rights and proceedings
Safeguard for existing human rights
11.   A person's reliance on a Convention right does not restrict–

> (a) any other right or freedom conferred on him by or under any law having effect in any part of the United Kingdom; or
>
> (b) his right to make any claim or bring any proceedings which he could make or bring apart from sections 7 to 9.

Freedom of expression
12. – (1) This section applies if a court is considering whether to grant any relief which, if granted, might affect the exercise of the Convention right to freedom of expression.

(2) If the person against whom the application for relief is made ("the respondent") is neither present nor represented, no such relief is to be granted unless the court is satisfied–

> (a) that the applicant has taken all practicable steps to notify the respondent; or
>
> (b) that there are compelling reasons why the respondent should not be notified.

(3) No such relief is to be granted so as to restrain publication before trial unless the court is satisfied that the applicant is likely to establish that publication should not be allowed.

(4) The court must have particular regard to the importance of the Convention right to freedom of expression and, where the proceedings relate to material which the respondent claims, or which appears to the court, to be journalistic, literary or artistic material (or to conduct connected with such material), to–
    (a) the extent to which–
        (i) the material has, or is about to, become available to the public; or
        (ii) it is, or would be, in the public interest for the material to be published;
    (b) any relevant privacy code.
(5) In this section–
"court" includes a tribunal; and
"relief" includes any remedy or order (other than in criminal proceedings).

Freedom of thought, conscience and religion
13. – (1) If a court's determination of any question arising under this Act might affect the exercise by a religious organisation (itself or its members collectively) of the Convention right to freedom of thought, conscience and religion, it must have particular regard to the importance of that right.
(2) In this section "court" includes a tribunal.

Derogations and reservations
Derogations
14. – (1) In this Act "designated derogation" means–
    (a) the United Kingdom's derogation from Article 5(3) of the Convention; and
    (b) any derogation by the United Kingdom from an Article of the Convention, or of any protocol to the Convention, which is designated for the purposes of this Act in an order made by the Secretary of State.
(2) The derogation referred to in subsection (1)(a) is set out in Part I of Schedule 3.
(3) If a designated derogation is amended or replaced it ceases to be a designated derogation.
(4) But subsection (3) does not prevent the Secretary of State from exercising his power under subsection (1)(b) to make a fresh designation order in respect of the Article concerned.
(5) The Secretary of State must by order make such amendments to Schedule 3 as he considers appropriate to reflect–
    (a) any designation order; or
    (b) the effect of subsection (3).
(6) A designation order may be made in anticipation of the making by

the United Kingdom of a proposed derogation.

Reservations

15. – (1) In this Act "designated reservation" means–

    (a) the United Kingdom's reservation to Article 2 of the First Protocol to the Convention; and

    (b) any other reservation by the United Kingdom to an Article of the Convention, or of any protocol to the Convention, which is designated for the purposes of this Act in an order made by the Secretary of State.

    (2) The text of the reservation referred to in subsection (1)(a) is set out in Part II of Schedule 3.

    (3) If a designated reservation is withdrawn wholly or in part it ceases to be a designated reservation.

    (4) But subsection (3) does not prevent the Secretary of State from exercising his power under subsection (1)(b) to make a fresh designation order in respect of the Article concerned.

    (5) The Secretary of State must by order make such amendments to this Act as he considers appropriate to reflect–

    (a) any designation order; or

    (b) the effect of subsection (3).

Period for designated derogations have effect

16. – (1) If it has not already been withdrawn by the United Kingdom, a designated derogation ceases to have effect for the purposes of this Act–

    (a) in the case of the derogation referred to in section 14(1)(a), at the end of the period of five years beginning with the date on which section 1(2) came into force;

    (b) in the case of any other derogation, at the end of the period of five years beginning with the date on which the order designating it was made.

    (2) At any time before the period–

    (a) fixed by subsection (1)(a) or (b), or

    (b) extended by an order under this subsection,

comes to an end, the Secretary of State may by order extend it by a further period of five years.

    (3) An order under section 14(1)(b) ceases to have effect at the end of the period for consideration, unless a resolution has been passed by each House approving the order.

    (4) Subsection (3) does not affect–

    (a) anything done in reliance on the order; or

    (b) the power to make a fresh order under section 14(1)(b).

    (5) In subsection (3) "period for consideration" means the period of forty days beginning with the day on which the order was made.

(6) In calculating the period for consideration, no account is to be taken of any time during which–
> (a) Parliament is dissolved or prorogued; or
> (b) both Houses are adjourned for more than four days.

(7) If a designated derogation is withdrawn by the United Kingdom, the Secretary of State must by order make such amendments to this Act as he considers are required to reflect that withdrawal.

Periodic review of designated reservations
17. – (1) The appropriate Minister must review the designated reservation referred to in section 15(1)(a)–
> (a) before the end of the period of five years beginning with the date on which section 1(2) came into force; and
> (b) if that designation is still in force, before the end of the period of five years beginning with the date on which the last report relating to it was laid under subsection (3).

(2) The appropriate Minister must review each of the other designated reservations (if any)–
> (a) before the end of the period of five years beginning with the date on which the order designating the reservation first came into force; and
> (b) if the designation is still in force, before the end of the period of five years beginning with the date on which the last report relating to it was laid under subsection (3).

(3) The Minister conducting a review under this section must prepare a report on the result of the review and lay a copy of it before each House of Parliament.

Judges of the European Court of Human Rights
Appointment to European Court of Human Rights
18. – (1) In this section "judicial office" means the office of–
> (a) Lord Justice of Appeal, Justice of the High Court or Circuit judge, in England and Wales;
> (b) judge of the Court of Session or sheriff, in Scotland;
> (c) Lord Justice of Appeal, judge of the High Court or county court judge, in Northern Ireland.

(2) The holder of a judicial office may become a judge of the European Court of Human Rights ("the Court") without being required to relinquish his office.

(3) But he is not required to perform the duties of his judicial office while he is a judge of the Court.

(4) In respect of any period during which he is a judge of the Court–
> (a) a Lord Justice of Appeal or Justice of the High Court is not to count as a judge of the relevant court for the purposes of sec-

tion 2(1) or 4(1) of the Supreme Court Act 1981 (maximum number of judges) nor as a judge of the Supreme Court for the purposes of section 12(1) to (6) of that Act (salaries etc.);
  (b) a judge of the Court of Session is not to count as a judge of that court for the purposes of section 1(1) of the Court of Session Act 1988 (maximum number of judges) or of section 9(1)(c) of the Administration of Justice Act 1973 ("the 1973 Act") (salaries etc.);
  (c) a Lord Justice of Appeal or judge of the High Court in Northern Ireland is not to count as a judge of the relevant court for the purposes of section 2(1) or 3(1) of the Judicature (Northern Ireland) Act 1978 (maximum number of judges) nor as a judge of the Supreme Court of Northern Ireland for the purposes of section 9(1)(d) of the 1973 Act (salaries etc.);
  (d) a Circuit judge is not to count as such for the purposes of section 18 of the Courts Act 1971 (salaries etc.);
  (e) a sheriff is not to count as such for the purposes of section 14 of the Sheriff Courts (Scotland) Act 1907 (salaries etc.);
  (f) a county court judge of Northern Ireland is not to count as such for the purposes of section 106 of the County Courts Act (Northern Ireland) 1959 (salaries etc.).

(5) If a sheriff principal is appointed a judge of the Court, section 11(1) of the Sheriff Courts (Scotland) Act 1971 (temporary appointment of sheriff principal) applies, while he holds that appointment, as if his office is vacant.

(6) Schedule 4 makes provision about judicial pensions in relation to the holder of a judicial office who serves as a judge of the Court.

(7) The Lord Chancellor or the Secretary of State may by order make such transitional provision (including, in particular, provision for a temporary increase in the maximum number of judges) as he considers appropriate in relation to any holder of a judicial office who has completed his service as a judge of the Court.

Parliamentary procedure
Statements of compatibility
19. – (1) A Minister of the Crown in charge of a Bill in either House of Parliament must, before Second Reading of the Bill–
  (a) make a statement to the effect that in his view the provisions of the Bill are compatible with the Convention rights ("a statement of compatibility"); or
  (b) make a statement to the effect that although he is unable to make a statement of compatibility the government nevertheless wishes the House to proceed with the Bill.

(2) The statement must be in writing and be published in such manner as the Minister making it considers appropriate.

Supplemental
Orders etc. under this Act
20. – (1) Any power of a Minister of the Crown to make an order under this Act is exercisable by statutory instrument.

(2) The power of the Lord Chancellor or the Secretary of State to make rules (other than rules of court) under section 2(3) or 7(9) is exercisable by statutory instrument.

(3) Any statutory instrument made under section 14, 15 or 16(7) must be laid before Parliament.

(4) No order may be made by the Lord Chancellor or the Secretary of State under section 1(4), 7(11) or 16(2) unless a draft of the order has been laid before, and approved by, each House of Parliament.

(5) Any statutory instrument made under section 18(7) or Schedule 4, or to which subsection (2) applies, shall be subject to annulment in pursuance of a resolution of either House of Parliament.

(6) The power of a Northern Ireland department to make–
    (a) rules under section 2(3)(c) or 7(9)(c), or
    (b) an order under section 7(11),
is exercisable by statutory rule for the purposes of the Statutory Rules (Northern Ireland) Order 1979.

(7) Any rules made under section 2(3)(c) or 7(9)(c) shall be subject to negative resolution; and section 41(6) of the Interpretation Act (Northern Ireland) 1954 (meaning of "subject to negative resolution") shall apply as if the power to make the rules were conferred by an Act of the Northern Ireland Assembly.

(8) No order may be made by a Northern Ireland department under section 7(11) unless a draft of the order has been laid before, and approved by, the Northern Ireland Assembly.

Interpretation, etc
21. – (1) In this Act–
    "amend" includes repeal and apply (with or without modifications);
    "the appropriate Minister" means the Minister of the Crown having charge of the appropriate authorised government department (within the meaning of the Crown Proceedings Act 1947);
    "the Commission" means the European Commission of Human Rights;
    "the Convention" means the Convention for the Protection of Human Rights and Fundamental Freedoms, agreed by the Council of Europe at Rome on 4th November 1950 as it has effect for the time being in relation to the United Kingdom;
    "declaration of incompatibility" means a declaration under section 4;
    "Minister of the Crown" has the same meaning as in the Ministers of the Crown Act 1975;
    "Northern Ireland Minister" includes the First Minister and the deputy

First Minister in Northern Ireland;
"primary legislation" means any–
(a) public general Act;
(b) local and personal Act;
(c) private Act;
(d) Measure of the Church Assembly;
(e) Measure of the General Synod of the Church of England;
(f) Order in Council–
   (i) made in exercise of Her Majesty's Royal Prerogative;
   (ii) made under section 38(1)(a) of the Northern Ireland Constitution Act 1973 or the corresponding provision of the Northern Ireland Act 1998; or
   (iii) amending an Act of a kind mentioned in paragraph (a), (b) or (c);

and includes an order or other instrument made under primary legislation (otherwise than by the National Assembly for Wales, a member of the Scottish Executive, a Northern Ireland Minister or a Northern Ireland department) to the extent to which it operates to bring one or more provisions of that legislation into force or amends any primary legislation;

"the First Protocol" means the protocol to the Convention agreed at Paris on 20th March 1952;

"the Sixth Protocol" means the protocol to the Convention agreed at Strasbourg on 28th April 1983;

"the Eleventh Protocol" means the protocol to the Convention (restructuring the control machinery established by the Convention) agreed at Strasbourg on 11th May 1994;

"remedial order" means an order under section 10;

"subordinate legislation" means any–
(a) Order in Council other than one–
   (i) made in exercise of Her Majesty's Royal Prerogative;
   (ii) made under section 38(1)(a) of the Northern Ireland Constitution Act 1973 or the corresponding provision of the Northern Ireland Act 1998; or
   (iii) amending an Act of a kind mentioned in the definition of primary legislation;
(b) Act of the Scottish Parliament;
(c) Act of the Parliament of Northern Ireland;
(d) Measure of the Assembly established under section 1 of the Northern Ireland Assembly Act 1973;
(e) Act of the Northern Ireland Assembly;
(f) order, rules, regulations, scheme, warrant, byelaw or other instrument made under primary legislation (except to the extent to which it operates to bring one or more provisions of that le-

gislation into force or amends any primary legislation);

(g) order, rules, regulations, scheme, warrant, byelaw or other instrument made under legislation mentioned in paragraph (b), (c), (d) or (e) or made under an Order in Council applying only to Northern Ireland;

(h) order, rules, regulations, scheme, warrant, byelaw or other instrument made by a member of the Scottish Executive, a Northern Ireland Minister or a Northern Ireland department in exercise of prerogative or other executive functions of Her Majesty which are exercisable by such a person on behalf of Her Majesty;

"transferred matters" has the same meaning as in the Northern Ireland Act 1998; and

"tribunal" means any tribunal in which legal proceedings may be brought.

(2) The references in paragraphs (b) and (c) of section 2(1) to Articles are to Articles of the Convention as they had effect immediately before the coming into force of the Eleventh Protocol.

(3) The reference in paragraph (d) of section 2(1) to Article 46 includes a reference to Articles 32 and 54 of the Convention as they had effect immediately before the coming into force of the Eleventh Protocol.

(4) The references in section 2(1) to a report or decision of the Commission or a decision of the Committee of Ministers include references to a report or decision made as provided by paragraphs 3, 4 and 6 of Article 5 of the Eleventh Protocol (transitional provisions).

(5) Any liability under the Army Act 1955, the Air Force Act 1955 or the Naval Discipline Act 1957 to suffer death for an offence is replaced by a liability to imprisonment for life or any less punishment authorised by those Acts; and those Acts shall accordingly have effect with the necessary modifications.

Short title, commencement, application and extent

22. – (1) This Act may be cited as the Human Rights Act 1998.

(2) Sections 18, 20 and 21(5) and this section come into force on the passing of this Act.

(3) The other provisions of this Act come into force on such day as the Secretary of State may by order appoint; and different days may be appointed for different purposes.

(4) Paragraph (b) of subsection (1) of section 7 applies to proceedings brought by or at the instigation of a public authority whenever the act in question took place; but otherwise that subsection does not apply to an act taking place before the coming into force of that section.

(5) This Act binds the Crown.

(6) This Act extends to Northern Ireland.

(7) Section 21(5), so far as it relates to any provision contained in the Army Act 1955, the Air Force Act 1955 or the Naval Discipline Act 1957, extends to any place to which that provision extends.

Schedules

Schedule 1: The Articles

Part I: The Convention
Rights and Freedoms

Article 2: Right to life

1. Everyone's right to life shall be protected by law. No one shall be deprived of his life intentionally save in the execution of a sentence of a court following his conviction of a crime for which this penalty is provided by law.

2. Deprivation of life shall not be regarded as inflicted in contravention of this Article when it results from the use of force which is no more than absolutely necessary:

   (a) in defence of any person from unlawful violence;
   (b) in order to effect a lawful arrest or to prevent the escape of a person lawfully detained;
   (c) in action lawfully taken for the purpose of quelling a riot or insurrection.

Article 3: Prohibition of torture

No one shall be subjected to torture or to inhuman or degrading treatment or punishment.

Article 4: Prohibition of slavery and forced labour

1. No one shall be held in slavery or servitude.

2. No one shall be required to perform forced or compulsory labour.

3. For the purpose of this Article the term "forced or compulsory labour" shall not include:

   (a) any work required to be done in the ordinary course of detention imposed according to the provisions of Article 5 of this Convention or during conditional release from such detention;
   (b) any service of a military character or, in case of conscientious objectors in countries where they are recognised, service exacted instead of compulsory military service;
   (c) any service exacted in case of an emergency or calamity threatening the life or well-being of the community;
   (d) any work or service which forms part of normal civic obligations.

Article 5: Right to liberty and security

1. Everyone has the right to liberty and security of person. No one shall be deprived of his liberty save in the following cases and in accordance with a

procedure prescribed by law:

(a) the lawful detention of a person after conviction by a competent court;

(b) the lawful arrest or detention of a person for non-compliance with the lawful order of a court or in order to secure the fulfilment of any obligation prescribed by law;

(c) the lawful arrest or detention of a person effected for the purpose of bringing him before the competent legal authority on reasonable suspicion of having committed an offence or when it is reasonably considered necessary to prevent his committing an offence or fleeing after having done so;

(d) the detention of a minor by lawful order for the purpose of educational supervision or his lawful detention for the purpose of bringing him before the competent legal authority;

(e) the lawful detention of persons for the prevention of the spreading of infectious diseases, of persons of unsound mind, alcoholics or drug addicts or vagrants;

(f) the lawful arrest or detention of a person to prevent his effecting an unauthorised entry into the country or of a person against whom action is being taken with a view to deportation or extradition.

2.   Everyone who is arrested shall be informed promptly, in a language which he understands, of the reasons for his arrest and of any charge against him.

3.   Everyone arrested or detained in accordance with the provisions of paragraph 1(c) of this Article shall be brought promptly before a judge or other officer authorised by law to exercise judicial power and shall be entitled to trial within a reasonable time or to release pending trial. Release may be conditioned by guarantees to appear for trial.

4.   Everyone who is deprived of his liberty by arrest or detention shall be entitled to take proceedings by which the lawfulness of his detention shall be decided speedily by a court and his release ordered if the detention is not lawful.

5.   Everyone who has been the victim of arrest or detention in contravention of the provisions of this Article shall have an enforceable right to compensation.

Article 6: Right to a fair trial

1.   In the determination of his civil rights and obligations or of any criminal charge against him, everyone is entitled to a fair and public hearing within a reasonable time by an independent and impartial tribunal established by law. Judgment shall be pronounced publicly but the press and public may be excluded from all or part of the trial in the interest of morals, public order or national security in a democratic society, where the interests of juveniles or the protection of the private life of the parties so require, or to the extent

strictly necessary in the opinion of the court in special circumstances where publicity would prejudice the interests of justice.

2.   Everyone charged with a criminal offence shall be presumed innocent until proved guilty according to law.

3.   Everyone charged with a criminal offence has the following minimum rights:

(a) to be informed promptly, in a language which he understands and in detail, of the nature and cause of the accusation against him;

(b) to have adequate time and facilities for the preparation of his defence;

(c) to defend himself in person or through legal assistance of his own choosing or, if he has not sufficient means to pay for legal assistance, to be given it free when the interests of justice so require;

(d) to examine or have examined witnesses against him and to obtain the attendance and examination of witnesses on his behalf under the same conditions as witnesses against him;

(e) to have the free assistance of an interpreter if he cannot understand or speak the language used in court.

Article 7: No punishment without law

1.   No one shall be held guilty of any criminal offence on account of any act or omission which did not constitute a criminal offence under national or international law at the time when it was committed. Nor shall a heavier penalty be imposed than the one that was applicable at the time the criminal offence was committed.

2.   This Article shall not prejudice the trial and punishment of any person for any act or omission which, at the time when it was committed, was criminal according to the general principles of law recognised by civilised nations.

Article 8: Right to respect for private and family life

1.   Everyone has the right to respect for his private and family life, his home and his correspondence.

2.   There shall be no interference by a public authority with the exercise of this right except such as is in accordance with the law and is necessary in a democratic society in the interests of national security, public safety or the economic well-being of the country, for the prevention of disorder or crime, for the protection of health or morals, or for the protection of the rights and freedoms of others.

Article 9: Freedom of thought, conscience and religion

1.   Everyone has the right to freedom of thought, conscience and religion; this right includes freedom to change his religion or belief and freedom, either alone or in community with others and in public or private, to manifest his religion or belief, in worship, teaching, practice and observance.

2.   Freedom to manifest one's religion or beliefs shall be subject only to such limitations as are prescribed by law and are necessary in a democratic society in the interests of public safety, for the protection of public order, health or morals, or for the protection of the rights and freedoms of others.

Article 10: Freedom of expression
1.   Everyone has the right to freedom of expression. This right shall include freedom to hold opinions and to receive and impart information and ideas without interference by public authority and regardless of frontiers. This Article shall not prevent States from requiring the licensing of broadcasting, television or cinema enterprises.
2.   The exercise of these freedoms, since it carries with it duties and responsibilities, may be subject to such formalities, conditions, restrictions or penalties as are prescribed by law and are necessary in a democratic society, in the interests of national security, territorial integrity or public safety, for the prevention of disorder or crime, for the protection of health or morals, for the protection of the reputation or rights of others, for preventing the disclosure of information received in confidence, or for maintaining the authority and impartiality of the judiciary.

Article 11: Freedom of assembly and association
1.   Everyone has the right to freedom of peaceful assembly and to freedom of association with others, including the right to form and to join trade unions for the protection of his interests.
2.   No restrictions shall be placed on the exercise of these rights other than such as are prescribed by law and are necessary in a democratic society in the interests of national security or public safety, for the prevention of disorder or crime, for the protection of health or morals or for the protection of the rights and freedoms of others. This Article shall not prevent the imposition of lawful restrictions on the exercise of these rights by members of the armed forces, of the police or of the administration of the State.

Article 12: Right to marry
Men and women of marriageable age have the right to marry and to found a family, according to the national laws governing the exercise of this right.

Article 14: Prohibition of discrimination
The enjoyment of the rights and freedoms set forth in this Convention shall be secured without discrimination on any ground such as sex, race, colour, language, religion, political or other opinion, national or social origin, association with a national minority, property, birth or other status.

Article 16: Restrictions on political activity of aliens
Nothing in Articles 10, 11 and 14 shall be regarded as preventing the High Contracting Parties from imposing restrictions on the political activity of aliens.

Article 17: Prohibition of abuse of rights

Nothing in this Convention may be interpreted as implying for any State, group or person any right to engage in any activity or perform any act aimed at the destruction of any of the rights and freedoms set forth herein or at their limitation to a greater extent than is provided for in the Convention.

Article 18: Limitation on use of restrictions on rights

The restrictions permitted under this Convention to the said rights and freedoms shall not be applied for any purpose other than those for which they have been prescribed.

Part II: The First Protocol

Article 1: Protection of property

Every natural or legal person is entitled to the peaceful enjoyment of his possessions. No one shall be deprived of his possessions except in the public interest and subject to the conditions provided for by law and by the general principles of international law.

The preceding provisions shall not, however, in any way impair the right of a State to enforce such laws as it deems necessary to control the use of property in accordance with the general interest or to secure the payment of taxes or other contributions or penalties.

Article 2: Right to education

No person shall be denied the right to education. In the exercise of any functions which it assumes in relation to education and to teaching, the State shall respect the right of parents to ensure such education and teaching in conformity with their own religious and philosophical convictions.

Article 3: Right to free elections

The High Contracting Parties undertake to hold free elections at reasonable intervals by secret ballot, under conditions which will ensure the free expression of the opinion of the people in the choice of the legislature.

Part III: The Sixth Protocol

Article 1: Abolition of the death penalty

The death penalty shall be abolished. No one shall be condemned to such penalty or executed.

Article 2: Death penalty in time of war

A State may make provision in its law for the death penalty in respect of acts committed in time of war or of imminent threat of war; such penalty shall be applied only in the instances laid down in the law and in accordance with its provisions. The State shall communicate to the Secretary General of the Council of Europe the relevant provisions of that law.

Schedule 2: Remedial Orders
Orders
1. – (1) A remedial order may–
    (a) contain such incidental, supplemental, consequential or trans-itional provision as the person making it considers appropriate;
    (b) be made so as to have effect from a date earlier than that on which it is made;
    (c) make provision for the delegation of specific functions;
    (d) make different provision for different cases.
  (2) The power conferred by sub-paragraph (1)(a) includes–
    (a) power to amend primary legislation (including primary legisla-tion other than that which contains the incompatible provision); and
    (b) power to amend or revoke subordinate legislation (including subordinate legislation other than that which contains the in-compatible provision).
  (3) A remedial order may be made so as to have the same extent as the legislation which it affects.
  (4) No person is to be guilty of an offence solely as a result of the retro-spective effect of a remedial order.

Procedure
2.   No remedial order may be made unless–
    (a) a draft of the order has been approved by a resolution of each House of Parliament made after the end of the period of 60 days beginning with the day on which the draft was laid; or
    (b) it is declared in the order that it appears to the person making it that, because of the urgency of the matter, it is necessary to make the order without a draft being so approved.

Orders laid in draft
3. – (1) No draft may be laid under paragraph 2(a) unless–
    (a) the person proposing to make the order has laid before Parlia-ment a document which contains a draft of the proposed order and the required information; and
    (b) the period of 60 days, beginning with the day on which the do-cument required by this sub-paragraph was laid, has ended.
  (2) If representations have been made during that period, the draft laid under paragraph 2(a) must be accompanied by a statement containing–
    (a) a summary of the representations; and
    (b) if, as a result of the representations, the proposed order has been changed, details of the changes.

Urgent cases
4. – (1) If a remedial order ("the original order") is made without being ap-

proved in draft, the person making it must lay it before Parliament, accompanied by the required information, after it is made.

(2) If representations have been made during the period of 60 days beginning with the day on which the original order was made, the person making it must (after the end of that period) lay before Parliament a statement containing–

    (a) a summary of the representations; and

    (b) if, as a result of the representations, he considers it appropriate to make changes to the original order, details of the changes.

(3) If sub-paragraph (2)(b) applies, the person making the statement must–

    (a) make a further remedial order replacing the original order; and

    (b) lay the replacement order before Parliament.

(4) If, at the end of the period of 120 days beginning with the day on which the original order was made, a resolution has not been passed by each House approving the original or replacement order, the order ceases to have effect (but without that affecting anything previously done under either order or the power to make a fresh remedial order).

Definitions
5.   In this Schedule–

"representations" means representations about a remedial order (or proposed remedial order) made to the person making (or proposing to make) it and includes any relevant Parliamentary report or resolution; and

"required information" means–

    (a) an explanation of the incompatibility which the order (or proposed order) seeks to remove, including particulars of the relevant declaration, finding or order; and

    (b) a statement of the reasons for proceeding under section 10 and for making an order in those terms.

Calculating periods
6.   In calculating any period for the purposes of this Schedule, no account is to be taken of any time during which–

    (a) Parliament is dissolved or prorogued; or

    (b) both Houses are adjourned for more than four days.

Schedule 3: Derogation and Reservation

Part I: Derogation

The 1988 notification
The United Kingdom Permanent Representative to the Council of Europe presents his compliments to the Secretary General of the Council, and has the honour to convey the following information in order to ensure com-

pliance with the obligations of Her Majesty's Government in the United Kingdom under Article 15(3) of the Convention for the Protection of Human Rights and Fundamental Freedoms signed at Rome on 4 November 1950.

There have been in the United Kingdom in recent years campaigns of organised terrorism connected with the affairs of Northern Ireland which have manifested themselves in activities which have included repeated murder, attempted murder, maiming, intimidation and violent civil disturbance and in bombing and fire raising which have resulted in death, injury and widespread destruction of property. As a result, a public emergency within the meaning of Article 15(1) of the Convention exists in the United Kingdom.

The Government found it necessary in 1974 to introduce and since then, in cases concerning persons reasonably suspected of involvement in terrorism connected with the affairs of Northern Ireland, or of certain offences under the legislation, who have been detained for 48 hours, to exercise powers enabling further detention without charge, for periods of up to five days, on the authority of the Secretary of State. These powers are at present to be found in Section 12 of the Prevention of Terrorism (Temporary Provisions) Act 1984, Article 9 of the Prevention of Terrorism (Supplemental Temporary Provisions) Order 1984 and Article 10 of the Prevention of Terrorism (Supplemental Temporary Provisions) (Northern Ireland) Order 1984.

Section 12 of the Prevention of Terrorism (Temporary Provisions) Act 1984 provides for a person whom a constable has arrested on reasonable grounds of suspecting him to be guilty of an offence under Section 1, 9 or 10 of the Act, or to be or to have been involved in terrorism connected with the affairs of Northern Ireland, to be detained in right of the arrest for up to 48 hours and thereafter, where the Secretary of State extends the detention period, for up to a further five days. Section 12 substantially re-enacted Section 12 of the Prevention of Terrorism (Temporary Provisions) Act 1976 which, in turn, substantially re-enacted Section 7 of the Prevention of Terrorism (Temporary Provisions) Act 1974.

Article 10 of the Prevention of Terrorism (Supplemental Temporary Provisions) (Northern Ireland) Order 1984 (SI 1984/417) and Article 9 of the Prevention of Terrorism (Supplemental Temporary Provisions) Order 1984 (SI 1984/418) were both made under Sections 13 and 14 of and Schedule 3 to the 1984 Act and substantially re-enacted powers of detention in Orders made under the 1974 and 1976 Acts. A person who is being examined under Article 4 of either Order on his arrival in, or on seeking to leave, Northern Ireland or Great Britain for the purpose of determining whether he is or has been involved in terrorism connected with the affairs of Northern Ireland, or whether there are grounds for suspecting that he has committed an offence under Section 9 of the 1984 Act, may be detained under Article 9 or 10, as appropriate, pending the conclusion of his examination. The period of this examination may exceed 12 hours if an examining officer has reasonable grounds for suspecting him to be or to have been involved in acts of terrorism connected with the affairs of Northern Ireland.

Where such a person is detained under the said Article 9 or 10 he may be detained for up to 48 hours on the authority of an examining officer and thereafter, where the Secretary of State extends the detention period, for up to a further five days.

In its judgment of 29 November 1988 in the Case of *Brogan and Others*, the European Court of Human Rights held that there had been a violation of Article 5(3) in respect of each of the applicants, all of whom had been detained under Section 12 of the 1984 Act. The Court held that even the shortest of the four periods of detention concerned, namely four days and six hours, fell outside the constraints as to time permitted by the first part of Article 5(3). In addition, the Court held that there had been a violation of Article 5(5) in the case of each applicant.

Following this judgment, the Secretary of State for the Home Department informed Parliament on 6 December 1988 that, against the background of the terrorist campaign, and the over-riding need to bring terrorists to justice, the Government did not believe that the maximum period of detention should be reduced. He informed Parliament that the Government were examining the matter with a view to responding to the judgment. On 22 December 1988, the Secretary of State further informed Parliament that it remained the Government's wish, if it could be achieved, to find a judicial process under which extended detention might be reviewed and where appropriate authorised by a judge or other judicial officer. But a further period of reflection and consultation was necessary before the Government could bring forward a firm and final view.

Since the judgment of 29 November 1988 as well as previously, the Government have found it necessary to continue to exercise, in relation to terrorism connected with the affairs of Northern Ireland, the powers described above enabling further detention without charge for periods of up to 5 days, on the authority of the Secretary of State, to the extent strictly required by the exigencies of the situation to enable necessary enquiries and investigations properly to be completed in order to decide whether criminal proceedings should be instituted. To the extent that the exercise of these powers may be inconsistent with the obligations imposed by the Convention the Government has availed itself of the right of derogation conferred by Article 15(1) of the Convention and will continue to do so until further notice. Dated 23 December 1988.

The 1989 notification

The United Kingdom Permanent Representative to the Council of Europe presents his compliments to the Secretary General of the Council, and has the honour to convey the following information.

In his communication to the Secretary General of 23 December 1988, reference was made to the introduction and exercise of certain powers under section 12 of the Prevention of Terrorism (Temporary Provisions) Act 1984, Article 9 of the Prevention of Terrorism (Supplemental Temporary Provisions) Order 1984 and Article 10 of the Prevention of Terrorism (Supplemental Temporary Provisions) (Northern Ireland) Order 1984.

These provisions have been replaced by section 14 of and paragraph 6 of Schedule 5 to the Prevention of Terrorism (Temporary Provisions) Act 1989, which make comparable provision. They came into force on 22 March 1989. A copy of these provisions is enclosed.

The United Kingdom Permanent Representative avails himself of this opportunity to renew to the Secretary General the assurance of his highest consideration.
23 March 1989.

Part II: Reservation

At the time of signing the present (First) Protocol, I declare that, in view of certain provisions of the Education Acts in the United Kingdom, the principle affirmed in the second sentence of Article 2 is accepted by the United Kingdom only so far as it is compatible with the provision of efficient instruction and training, and the avoidance of unreasonable public expenditure. Dated 20 March 1952. Made by the United Kingdom Permanent Representative to the Council of Europe.

Schedule 4: Judicial Pensions
Duty to make orders about pensions
1. – (1) The appropriate Minister must by order make provision with respect to pensions payable to or in respect of any holder of a judicial office who serves as an ECHR judge.

(2) A pensions order must include such provision as the Minister making it considers is necessary to secure that–
  (a) an ECHR judge who was, immediately before his appointment as an ECHR judge, a member of a judicial pension scheme is entitled to remain as a member of that scheme;
  (b) the terms on which he remains a member of the scheme are those which would have been applicable had he not been appointed as an ECHR judge; and
  (c) entitlement to benefits payable in accordance with the scheme continues to be determined as if, while serving as an ECHR judge, his salary was that which would (but for section 18(4)) have been payable to him in respect of his continuing service as the holder of his judicial office.

Contributions

2.   A pensions order may, in particular, make provision–
>   (a) for any contributions which are payable by a person who re-
>   mains a member of a scheme as a result of the order, and which
>   would otherwise be payable by deduction from his salary, to be
>   made otherwise than by deduction from his salary as an ECHR
>   judge; and
>   (b) for such contributions to be collected in such manner as may be
>   determined by the administrators of the scheme.

Amendments of other enactments

3.   A pensions order may amend any provision of, or made under, a pensions Act in such manner and to such extent as the Minister making the order
considers necessary or expedient to ensure the proper administration of any
scheme to which it relates.

Definitions

4.   In this Schedule–
>   "appropriate Minister" means–
>   (a) in relation to any judicial office whose jurisdiction is exercis-
>   able exclusively in relation to Scotland, the Secretary of State;
>   and
>   (b) otherwise, the Lord Chancellor;

"ECHR judge" means the holder of a judicial office who is serving as a
judge of the Court;

"judicial pension scheme" means a scheme established by and in accordance with a pensions Act;

"pensions Act" means–
>   (a) the County Courts Act (Northern Ireland) 1959;
>   (b) the Sheriffs' Pensions (Scotland) Act 1961;
>   (c) the Judicial Pensions Act 1981; or
>   (d) the Judicial Pensions and Retirement Act 1993; and

"pensions order" means an order made under paragraph 1.

Appendix 2

The Convention for the Protection of Human Rights and Fundamental Freedoms

Rome, 4.XI.1950

[Source: www.echr.coe.int]

The text of the Convention had been amended according to the provisions of Protocol No. 3 (ETS No. 45), which entered into force on 21 September 1970, of Protocol No. 5 (ETS No. 55), which entered into force on 20 December 1971 and of Protocol No. 8 (ETS No. 118), which entered into force on 1 January 1990, and comprised also the text of Protocol No. 2 (ETS No. 44) which, in accordance with Article 5, paragraph 3 thereof, had been an integral part of the Convention since its entry into force on 21 September 1970. All provisions which had been amended or added by these Protocols are replaced by Protocol No. 11 (ETS No. 155), as from the date of its entry into force on 1 November 1998. As from that date, Protocol n° 9 (ETS No. 140), which entered into force on 1 October 1994, is repealed and Protocol n° 10 (ETS No. 146), which has not entered into force, has lost its purpose.

The governments signatory hereto, being members of the Council of Europe,

Considering the Universal Declaration of Human Rights proclaimed by the General Assembly of the United Nations on 10th December 1948;

Considering that this Declaration aims at securing the universal and effective recognition and observance of the Rights therein declared;

Considering that the aim of the Council of Europe is the achievement of greater unity between its members and that one of the methods by which that aim is to be pursued is the maintenance and further realisation of human rights and fundamental freedoms;

Reaffirming their profound belief in those fundamental freedoms which are the foundation of justice and peace in the world and are best maintained on the one hand by an effective political democracy and on the other by a common understanding and observance of the human rights upon which they depend;

Being resolved, as the governments of European countries which are

like-minded and have a common heritage of political traditions, ideals, freedom and the rule of law, to take the first steps for the collective enforcement of certain of the rights stated in the Universal Declaration,
Have agreed as follows:

Article 1: Obligation to respect human rights [1]
The High Contracting Parties shall secure to everyone within their jurisdiction the rights and freedoms defined in Section I of this Convention.

Section I: Rights and freedoms

Article 2: Right to life [1]
1   Everyone's right to life shall be protected by law. No one shall be deprived of his life intentionally save in the execution of a sentence of a court following his conviction of a crime for which this penalty is provided by law.
2   Deprivation of life shall not be regarded as inflicted in contravention of this article when it results from the use of force which is no more than absolutely necessary:
    a   in defence of any person from unlawful violence;
    b   in order to effect a lawful arrest or to prevent the escape of a person lawfully detained;
    c   in action lawfully taken for the purpose of quelling a riot or insurrection.

Article 3: Prohibition of torture [1]
No one shall be subjected to torture or to inhuman or degrading treatment or punishment.

Article 4: Prohibition of slavery and forced labour [1]
1   No one shall be held in slavery or servitude.
2   No one shall be required to perform forced or compulsory labour.
3   For the purpose of this article the term "forced or compulsory labour" shall not include:
    a   any work required to be done in the ordinary course of detention imposed according to the provisions of Article 5 of this Convention or during conditional release from such detention;
    b   any service of a military character or, in case of conscientious objectors in countries where they are recognised, service exacted instead of compulsory military service;
    c   any service exacted in case of an emergency or calamity threatening the life or well-being of the community;
    d   any work or service which forms part of normal civic obligations.

Article 5: Right to liberty and security [1]
1   Everyone has the right to liberty and security of person. No one shall be

deprived of his liberty save in the following cases and in accordance with a procedure prescribed by law:

  a   the lawful detention of a person after conviction by a competent court;

  b   the lawful arrest or detention of a person for non-compliance with the lawful order of a court or in order to secure the fulfilment of any obligation prescribed by law;

  c   the lawful arrest or detention of a person effected for the purpose of bringing him before the competent legal authority on reasonable suspicion of having committed an offence or when it is reasonably considered necessary to prevent his committing an offence or fleeing after having done so;

  d   the detention of a minor by lawful order for the purpose of educational supervision or his lawful detention for the purpose of bringing him before the competent legal authority;

  e   the lawful detention of persons for the prevention of the spreading of infectious diseases, of persons of unsound mind, alcoholics or drug addicts or vagrants;

  f   the lawful arrest or detention of a person to prevent his effecting an unauthorised entry into the country or of a person against whom action is being taken with a view to deportation or extradition.

2   Everyone who is arrested shall be informed promptly, in a language which he understands, of the reasons for his arrest and of any charge against him.

3   Everyone arrested or detained in accordance with the provisions of paragraph 1.c of this article shall be brought promptly before a judge or other officer authorised by law to exercise judicial power and shall be entitled to trial within a reasonable time or to release pending trial. Release may be conditioned by guarantees to appear for trial.

4   Everyone who is deprived of his liberty by arrest or detention shall be entitled to take proceedings by which the lawfulness of his detention shall be decided speedily by a court and his release ordered if the detention is not lawful.

5   Everyone who has been the victim of arrest or detention in contravention of the provisions of this article shall have an enforceable right to compensation.

Article 6: Right to a fair trial [1]

1   In the determination of his civil rights and obligations or of any criminal charge against him, everyone is entitled to a fair and public hearing within a reasonable time by an independent and impartial tribunal established by law. Judgment shall be pronounced publicly but the press and public may be excluded from all or part of the trial in the interests of morals, public order or national security in a democratic society, where the interests of juveniles

or the protection of the private life of the parties so require, or to the extent strictly necessary in the opinion of the court in special circumstances where publicity would prejudice the interests of justice.

2   Everyone charged with a criminal offence shall be presumed innocent until proved guilty according to law.

3   Everyone charged with a criminal offence has the following minimum rights:

    a   to be informed promptly, in a language which he understands and in detail, of the nature and cause of the accusation against him;

    b   to have adequate time and facilities for the preparation of his defence;

    c   to defend himself in person or through legal assistance of his own choosing or, if he has not sufficient means to pay for legal assistance, to be given it free when the interests of justice so require;

    d   to examine or have examined witnesses against him and to obtain the attendance and examination of witnesses on his behalf under the same conditions as witnesses against him;

    e   to have the free assistance of an interpreter if he cannot understand or speak the language used in court.

Article 7: No punishment without law [1]

1   No one shall be held guilty of any criminal offence on account of any act or omission which did not constitute a criminal offence under national or international law at the time when it was committed. Nor shall a heavier penalty be imposed than the one that was applicable at the time the criminal offence was committed.

2   This article shall not prejudice the trial and punishment of any person for any act or omission which, at the time when it was committed, was criminal according to the general principles of law recognised by civilised nations.

Article 8: Right to respect for private and family life [1]

1   Everyone has the right to respect for his private and family life, his home and his correspondence.

2   There shall be no interference by a public authority with the exercise of this right except such as is in accordance with the law and is necessary in a democratic society in the interests of national security, public safety or the economic well-being of the country, for the prevention of disorder or crime, for the protection of health or morals, or for the protection of the rights and freedoms of others.

Article 9: Freedom of thought, conscience and religion [1]

1   Everyone has the right to freedom of thought, conscience and religion; this right includes freedom to change his religion or belief and freedom, either alone or in community with others and in public or private, to manifest

his religion or belief, in worship, teaching, practice and observance.

2   Freedom to manifest one's religion or beliefs shall be subject only to such limitations as are prescribed by law and are necessary in a democratic society in the interests of public safety, for the protection of public order, health or morals, or for the protection of the rights and freedoms of others.

Article 10: Freedom of expression [1]

1   Everyone has the right to freedom of expression. This right shall include freedom to hold opinions and to receive and impart information and ideas without interference by public authority and regardless of frontiers. This article shall not prevent States from requiring the licensing of broadcasting, television or cinema enterprises.

2   The exercise of these freedoms, since it carries with it duties and responsibilities, may be subject to such formalities, conditions, restrictions or penalties as are prescribed by law and are necessary in a democratic society, in the interests of national security, territorial integrity or public safety, for the prevention of disorder or crime, for the protection of health or morals, for the protection of the reputation or rights of others, for preventing the disclosure of information received in confidence, or for maintaining the authority and impartiality of the judiciary.

Article 11: Freedom of assembly and association [1]

1   Everyone has the right to freedom of peaceful assembly and to freedom of association with others, including the right to form and to join trade unions for the protection of his interests.

2   No restrictions shall be placed on the exercise of these rights other than such as are prescribed by law and are necessary in a democratic society in the interests of national security or public safety, for the prevention of disorder or crime, for the protection of health or morals or for the protection of the rights and freedoms of others. This article shall not prevent the imposition of lawful restrictions on the exercise of these rights by members of the armed forces, of the police or of the administration of the State.

Article 12: Right to marry [1]

Men and women of marriageable age have the right to marry and to found a family, according to the national laws governing the exercise of this right.

Article 13: Right to an effective remedy [1]

Everyone whose rights and freedoms as set forth in this Convention are violated shall have an effective remedy before a national authority notwithstanding that the violation has been committed by persons acting in an official capacity.

Article 14: Prohibition of discrimination [1]

The enjoyment of the rights and freedoms set forth in this Convention shall be secured without discrimination on any ground such as sex, race, colour, language, religion, political or other opinion, national or social origin, association with a national minority, property, birth or other status.

Article 15: Derogation in time of emergency [1]

1   In time of war or other public emergency threatening the life of the nation any High Contracting Party may take measures derogating from its obligations under this Convention to the extent strictly required by the exigencies of the situation, provided that such measures are not inconsistent with its other obligations under international law.

2   No derogation from Article 2, except in respect of deaths resulting from lawful acts of war, or from Articles 3, 4 (paragraph 1) and 7 shall be made under this provision.

3   Any High Contracting Party availing itself of this right of derogation shall keep the Secretary General of the Council of Europe fully informed of the measures which it has taken and the reasons therefor. It shall also inform the Secretary General of the Council of Europe when such measures have ceased to operate and the provisions of the Convention are again being fully executed.

Article 16: Restrictions on political activity of aliens [1]

Nothing in Articles 10, 11 and 14 shall be regarded as preventing the High Contracting Parties from imposing restrictions on the political activity of aliens.

Article 17: Prohibition of abuse of rights [1]

Nothing in this Convention may be interpreted as implying for any State, group or person any right to engage in any activity or perform any act aimed at the destruction of any of the rights and freedoms set forth herein or at their limitation to a greater extent than is provided for in the Convention.

Article 18: Limitation on use of restrictions on rights [1]

The restrictions permitted under this Convention to the said rights and freedoms shall not be applied for any purpose other than those for which they have been prescribed.

Section II – European Court of Human Rights [2]

Article 19: Establishment of the Court

To ensure the observance of the engagements undertaken by the High Contracting Parties in the Convention and the Protocols thereto, there shall be set up a European Court of Human Rights, hereinafter referred to as "the Court". It shall function on a permanent basis.

Article 20: Number of judges

The Court shall consist of a number of judges equal to that of the High Contracting Parties.

Article 21: Criteria for office

1   The judges shall be of high moral character and must either possess the qualifications required for appointment to high judicial office or be jurisconsults of recognised competence.

2   The judges shall sit on the Court in their individual capacity.

3   During their term of office the judges shall not engage in any activity which is incompatible with their independence, impartiality or with the demands of a full-time office; all questions arising from the application of this paragraph shall be decided by the Court.

Article 22: Election of judges

1   The judges shall be elected by the Parliamentary Assembly with respect to each High Contracting Party by a majority of votes cast from a list of three candidates nominated by the High Contracting Party.

2   The same procedure shall be followed to complete the Court in the event of the accession of new High Contracting Parties and in filling casual vacancies.

Article 23: Terms of office

1   The judges shall be elected for a period of six years. They may be re-elected. However, the terms of office of one-half of the judges elected at the first election shall expire at the end of three years.

2   The judges whose terms of office are to expire at the end of the initial period of three years shall be chosen by lot by the Secretary General of the Council of Europe immediately after their election.

3   In order to ensure that, as far as possible, the terms of office of one-half of the judges are renewed every three years, the Parliamentary Assembly may decide, before proceeding to any subsequent election, that the term or terms of office of one or more judges to be elected shall be for a period other than six years but not more than nine and not less than three years.

4   In cases where more than one term of office is involved and where the Parliamentary Assembly applies the preceding paragraph, the allocation of the terms of office shall be effected by a drawing of lots by the Secretary General of the Council of Europe immediately after the election.

5   A judge elected to replace a judge whose term of office has not expired shall hold office for the remainder of his predecessor's term.

6   The terms of office of judges shall expire when they reach the age of 70.

7   The judges shall hold office until replaced. They shall, however, continue to deal with such cases as they already have under consideration.

Article 24: Dismissal

No judge may be dismissed from his office unless the other judges decide by a majority of two-thirds that he has ceased to fulfil the required conditions.

Article 25: Registry and legal secretaries
The Court shall have a registry, the functions and organisation of which shall be laid down in the rules of the Court. The Court shall be assisted by legal secretaries.

Article 26: Plenary Court
The plenary Court shall
    a   elect its President and one or two Vice-Presidents for a period of three years; they may be re-elected;
    b   set up Chambers, constituted for a fixed period of time;
    c   elect the Presidents of the Chambers of the Court; they may be re-elected;
    d   adopt the rules of the Court, and
    e   elect the Registrar and one or more Deputy Registrars.

Article 27: Committees, Chambers and Grand Chamber
1   To consider cases brought before it, the Court shall sit in committees of three judges, in Chambers of seven judges and in a Grand Chamber of seventeen judges. The Court's Chambers shall set up committees for a fixed period of time.
2   There shall sit as an *ex officio* member of the Chamber and the Grand Chamber the judge elected in respect of the State Party concerned or, if there is none or if he is unable to sit, a person of its choice who shall sit in the capacity of judge.
3   The Grand Chamber shall also include the President of the Court, the Vice-Presidents, the Presidents of the Chambers and other judges chosen in accordance with the rules of the Court. When a case is referred to the Grand Chamber under Article 43, no judge from the Chamber which rendered the judgment shall sit in the Grand Chamber, with the exception of the President of the Chamber and the judge who sat in respect of the State Party concerned.

Article 28: Declarations of inadmissibility by committees
A committee may, by a unanimous vote, declare inadmissible or strike out of its list of cases an application submitted under Article 34 where such a decision can be taken without further examination. The decision shall be final.

Article 29: Decisions by Chambers on admissibility and merits
1   If no decision is taken under Article 28, a Chamber shall decide on the admissibility and merits of individual applications submitted under Article 34.
2   A Chamber shall decide on the admissibility and merits of inter-State applications submitted under Article 33.
3   The decision on admissibility shall be taken separately unless the Court, in exceptional cases, decides otherwise.

Article 30: Relinquishment of jurisdiction to the Grand Chamber
Where a case pending before a Chamber raises a serious question affecting the interpretation of the Convention or the protocols thereto, or where the resolution of a question before the Chamber might have a result inconsistent with a judgment previously delivered by the Court, the Chamber may, at any time before it has rendered its judgment, relinquish jurisdiction in favour of the Grand Chamber, unless one of the parties to the case objects.

Article 31: Powers of the Grand Chamber
The Grand Chamber shall
    a   determine applications submitted either under Article 33 or Article 34 when a Chamber has relinquished jurisdiction under Article 30 or when the case has been referred to it under Article 43; and
    b   consider requests for advisory opinions submitted under Article 47.

Article 32: Jurisdiction of the Court
1   The jurisdiction of the Court shall extend to all matters concerning the interpretation and application of the Convention and the protocols thereto which are referred to it as provided in Articles 33, 34 and 47.
2   In the event of dispute as to whether the Court has jurisdiction, the Court shall decide.

Article 33: Inter-State cases
Any High Contracting Party may refer to the Court any alleged breach of the provisions of the Convention and the protocols thereto by another High Contracting Party.

Article 34: Individual applications
The Court may receive applications from any person, non-governmental organisation or group of individuals claiming to be the victim of a violation by one of the High Contracting Parties of the rights set forth in the Convention or the protocols thereto. The High Contracting Parties undertake not to hinder in any way the effective exercise of this right.

Article 35: Admissibility criteria
1   The Court may only deal with the matter after all domestic remedies have been exhausted, according to the generally recognised rules of international law, and within a period of six months from the date on which the final decision was taken.
2   The Court shall not deal with any application submitted under Article 34 that
    a   is anonymous; or
    b   is substantially the same as a matter that has already been examined by the Court or has already been submitted to another procedure of international investigation or settlement and contains no relevant new information.

3   The Court shall declare inadmissible any individual application submitted under Article 34 which it considers incompatible with the provisions of the Convention or the protocols thereto, manifestly ill-founded, or an abuse of the right of application.
4   The Court shall reject any application which it considers inadmissible under this Article. It may do so at any stage of the proceedings.

Article 36: Third party intervention
1   In all cases before a Chamber or the Grand Chamber, a High Contracting Party one of whose nationals is an applicant shall have the right to submit written comments and to take part in hearings.
2   The President of the Court may, in the interest of the proper administration of justice, invite any High Contracting Party which is not a party to the proceedings or any person concerned who is not the applicant to submit written comments or take part in hearings.

Article 37: Striking out applications
1   The Court may at any stage of the proceedings decide to strike an application out of its list of cases where the circumstances lead to the conclusion that
    a   the applicant does not intend to pursue his application; or
    b   the matter has been resolved; or
    c   for any other reason established by the Court, it is no longer justified to continue the examination of the application.
However, the Court shall continue the examination of the application if respect for human rights as defined in the Convention and the protocols thereto so requires.
2   The Court may decide to restore an application to its list of cases if it considers that the circumstances justify such a course.

Article 38: Examination of the case and friendly settlement proceedings
1   If the Court declares the application admissible, it shall
    a   pursue the examination of the case, together with the representatives of the parties, and if need be, undertake an investigation, for the effective conduct of which the States concerned shall furnish all necessary facilities;
    b   place itself at the disposal of the parties concerned with a view to securing a friendly settlement of the matter on the basis of respect for human rights as defined in the Convention and the protocols thereto.
2   Proceedings conducted under paragraph 1.b shall be confidential.

Article 39: Finding of a friendly settlement
If a friendly settlement is effected, the Court shall strike the case out of its list by means of a decision which shall be confined to a brief statement of

the facts and of the solution reached.

Article 40: Public hearings and access to documents

1   Hearings shall be in public unless the Court in exceptional circumstances decides otherwise.

2   Documents deposited with the Registrar shall be accessible to the public unless the President of the Court decides otherwise.

Article 41: Just satisfaction

If the Court finds that there has been a violation of the Convention or the protocols thereto, and if the internal law of the High Contracting Party concerned allows only partial reparation to be made, the Court shall, if necessary, afford just satisfaction to the injured party.

Article 42: Judgments of Chambers

Judgments of Chambers shall become final in accordance with the provisions of Article 44, paragraph 2.

Article 43: Referral to the Grand Chamber

1   Within a period of three months from the date of the judgment of the Chamber, any party to the case may, in exceptional cases, request that the case be referred to the Grand Chamber.

2   A panel of five judges of the Grand Chamber shall accept the request if the case raises a serious question affecting the interpretation or application of the Convention or the protocols thereto, or a serious issue of general importance.

3   If the panel accepts the request, the Grand Chamber shall decide the case by means of a judgment.

Article 44: Final judgments

1   The judgment of the Grand Chamber shall be final.

2   The judgment of a Chamber shall become final

   a   when the parties declare that they will not request that the case be referred to the Grand Chamber; or

   b   three months after the date of the judgment, if reference of the case to the Grand Chamber has not been requested; or

   c   when the panel of the Grand Chamber rejects the request to refer under Article 43.

3   The final judgment shall be published.

Article 45: Reasons for judgments and decisions

1   Reasons shall be given for judgments as well as for decisions declaring applications admissible or inadmissible.

2   If a judgment does not represent, in whole or in part, the unanimous opinion of the judges, any judge shall be entitled to deliver a separate opinion.

Article 46: Binding force and execution of judgments
1   The High Contracting Parties undertake to abide by the final judgment of the Court in any case to which they are parties.
2   The final judgment of the Court shall be transmitted to the Committee of Ministers, which shall supervise its execution.

Article 47: Advisory opinions
1   The Court may, at the request of the Committee of Ministers, give advisory opinions on legal questions concerning the interpretation of the Convention and the protocols thereto.
2   Such opinions shall not deal with any question relating to the content or scope of the rights or freedoms defined in Section I of the Convention and the protocols thereto, or with any other question which the Court or the Committee of Ministers might have to consider in consequence of any such proceedings as could be instituted in accordance with the Convention.
3   Decisions of the Committee of Ministers to request an advisory opinion of the Court shall require a majority vote of the representatives entitled to sit on the Committee.

Article 48: Advisory jurisdiction of the Court
The Court shall decide whether a request for an advisory opinion submitted by the Committee of Ministers is within its competence as defined in Article 47.

Article 49: Reasons for advisory opinions
1   Reasons shall be given for advisory opinions of the Court.
2   If the advisory opinion does not represent, in whole or in part, the unanimous opinion of the judges, any judge shall be entitled to deliver a separate opinion.
3   Advisory opinions of the Court shall be communicated to the Committee of Ministers.

Article 50: Expenditure on the Court
The expenditure on the Court shall be borne by the Council of Europe.

Article 51: Privileges and immunities of judges
The judges shall be entitled, during the exercise of their functions, to the privileges and immunities provided for in Article 40 of the Statute of the Council of Europe and in the agreements made thereunder.

Section III: Miscellaneous provisions [3,1]

Article 52: Inquiries by the Secretary General [1]
On receipt of a request from the Secretary General of the Council of Europe any High Contracting Party shall furnish an explanation of the manner in which its internal law ensures the effective implementation of any of the pro-

visions of the Convention.

Article 53: Safeguard for existing human rights [1]
Nothing in this Convention shall be construed as limiting or derogating from any of the human rights and fundamental freedoms which may be ensured under the laws of any High Contracting Party or under any other agreement to which it is a Party.

Article 54: Powers of the Committee of Ministers [1]
Nothing in this Convention shall prejudice the powers conferred on the Committee of Ministers by the Statute of the Council of Europe.

Article 55: Exclusion of other means of dispute settlement [1]
The High Contracting Parties agree that, except by special agreement, they will not avail themselves of treaties, conventions or declarations in force between them for the purpose of submitting, by way of petition, a dispute arising out of the interpretation or application of this Convention to a means of settlement other than those provided for in this Convention.

Article 56: Territorial application [1]
1 [4] Any State may at the time of its ratification or at any time thereafter declare by notification addressed to the Secretary General of the Council of Europe that the present Convention shall, subject to paragraph 4 of this Article, extend to all or any of the territories for whose international relations it is responsible.
2 The Convention shall extend to the territory or territories named in the notification as from the thirtieth day after the receipt of this notification by the Secretary General of the Council of Europe.
3 The provisions of this Convention shall be applied in such territories with due regard, however, to local requirements.
4 [4] Any State which has made a declaration in accordance with paragraph 1 of this article may at any time thereafter declare on behalf of one or more of the territories to which the declaration relates that it accepts the competence of the Court to receive applications from individuals, non-governmental organisations or groups of individuals as provided by Article 34 of the Convention.

Article 57: Reservations [1]
1 Any State may, when signing this Convention or when depositing its instrument of ratification, make a reservation in respect of any particular provision of the Convention to the extent that any law then in force in its territory is not in conformity with the provision. Reservations of a general character shall not be permitted under this article.
2 Any reservation made under this article shall contain a brief statement of the law concerned.

Article 58: Denunciation [1]

1   A High Contracting Party may denounce the present Convention only after the expiry of five years from the date on which it became a party to it and after six months' notice contained in a notification addressed to the Secretary General of the Council of Europe, who shall inform the other High Contracting Parties.

2   Such a denunciation shall not have the effect of releasing the High Contracting Party concerned from its obligations under this Convention in respect of any act which, being capable of constituting a violation of such obligations, may have been performed by it before the date at which the denunciation became effective.

3   Any High Contracting Party which shall cease to be a member of the Council of Europe shall cease to be a Party to this Convention under the same conditions.

4 [4]   The Convention may be denounced in accordance with the provisions of the preceding paragraphs in respect of any territory to which it has been declared to extend under the terms of Article 56.

Article 59: Signature and ratification [1]

1   This Convention shall be open to the signature of the members of the Council of Europe. It shall be ratified. Ratifications shall be deposited with the Secretary General of the Council of Europe.

2   The present Convention shall come into force after the deposit of ten instruments of ratification.

3   As regards any signatory ratifying subsequently, the Convention shall come into force at the date of the deposit of its instrument of ratification.

4   The Secretary General of the Council of Europe shall notify all the members of the Council of Europe of the entry into force of the Convention, the names of the High Contracting Parties who have ratified it, and the deposit of all instruments of ratification which may be effected subsequently.

Done at Rome this 4th day of November 1950, in English and French, both texts being equally authentic, in a single copy which shall remain deposited in the archives of the Council of Europe. The Secretary General shall transmit certified copies to each of the signatories.

[1]   Heading added according to the provisions of Protocol No. 11 (ETS No. 155).

[2]   New Section II according to the provisions of Protocol No. 11 (ETS No. 155).

[3]   The articles of this Section are renumbered according to the provisions of Protocol No. 11 (ETS No. 155).

[4]   Text amended according to the provisions of Protocol No. 11 (ETS No. 155).

Index